THE BEDFORD SERIES IN HISTORY AND CULTURE

The Lancaster Treaty
of 1744

with Related Documents

Related Titles in
THE BEDFORD SERIES IN HISTORY AND CULTURE
Advisory Editors: Lynn Hunt, *University of California, Los Angeles*
David W. Blight, *Yale University*
Bonnie G. Smith, *Rutgers University*
Natalie Zemon Davis, *Princeton University*
Ernest R. May, *Harvard University*

Christopher Columbus and the Enterprise of the Indies: A Brief History with Documents
Geoffrey Symcox, *University of California, Los Angeles*, and Blair Sullivan, *University of California, Los Angeles*

Victors and Vanquished: Spanish and Nahua Views of the Conquest of Mexico
Edited with an Introduction by Stuart B. Schwartz, *Yale University*

Envisioning America: English Plans for the Colonization of North America, 1580–1640
Edited with an Introduction by Peter C. Mancall, *University of Southern California*

THE JESUIT RELATIONS: *Natives and Missionaries in Seventeenth-Century North America*
Edited with an Introduction by Allan Greer, *University of Toronto*

THE SOVEREIGNTY AND GOODNESS OF GOD *by Mary Rowlandson with Related Documents*
Edited with an Introduction by Neal Salisbury, *Smith College*

The World Turned Upside Down: Indian Voices from Early America
Edited with an Introduction by Colin G. Calloway, *Dartmouth College*

THE AUTOBIOGRAPHY OF BENJAMIN FRANKLIN *with Related Documents*, Second Edition
Edited with an Introduction by Louis P. Masur, *City College of the City University of New York*

The Lewis and Clark Expedition: Selections from the Journals, Arranged by Topic
Edited with an Introduction by Gunther Barth, *University of California, Berkeley*

The Cherokee Removal: A Brief History with Documents, Second Edition
Theda Perdue and Michael D. Green, *University of North Carolina at Chapel Hill*

Our Hearts Fell to the Ground: Plains Indian Views of How the West Was Lost
Edited with an Introduction by Colin G. Calloway, *Dartmouth College*

Talking Back to Civilization: Indian Voices from the Progressive Era
Edited with an Introduction by Frederick E. Hoxie, *University of Illinois at Urbana-Champaign*

THE BEDFORD SERIES IN HISTORY AND CULTURE

The Lancaster Treaty
of 1744
with Related Documents

Edited with an Introduction by

James H. Merrell
Vassar College

BEDFORD/ST. MARTIN'S   Boston ♦ New York

To the students I have worked with at Vassar College

For Bedford/St. Martin's

Publisher for History: Mary V. Dougherty
Director of Development: Jane Knetzger
Developmental Editor: Kathryn Abbott
Editorial Assistants: Laurel Damashek, Katherine Flynn
Production Supervisor: Jennifer Peterson
Production Assistant: Sarah Ulicny
Executive Marketing Manager: Jenna Bookin Barry
Project Management: Books By Design, Inc.
Text Design: Claire Seng-Niemoeller
Index: Books By Design, Inc.
Cover Design: Liz Tardiff
Cover Art: *The Indians Giving a Talk to Colonel Bouquet . . . in October 1764*, by Benjamin West. Rosenbach Museum and Library
Composition: Stratford/TexTech
Printing and Binding: RR Donnelley & Sons Company

President: Joan E. Feinberg
Editorial Director: Denise B. Wydra
Director of Marketing: Karen Melton Soeltz
Director of Editing, Design, and Production: Marcia Cohen
Assistant Director of Editing, Design, and Production: Elise S. Kaiser
Manager, Publishing Services: Emily Berleth

Library of Congress Control Number: 2007932897

Manufactured in the United States of America.

2 1 0 9 8 7
f e d c b a

For information, write: Bedford/St. Martin's, 75 Arlington Street, Boston, MA 02116 (617-399-4000)

ISBN-10: 0-312-45414-7
ISBN-13: 978-0-312-45414-2

Foreword

The Bedford Series in History and Culture is designed so that readers can study the past as historians do.

The historian's first task is finding the evidence. Documents, letters, memoirs, interviews, pictures, movies, novels, or poems can provide facts and clues. Then the historian questions and compares the sources. There is more to do than in a courtroom, for hearsay evidence is welcome, and the historian is usually looking for answers beyond act and motive. Different views of an event may be as important as a single verdict. How a story is told may yield as much information as what it says.

Along the way the historian seeks help from other historians and perhaps from specialists in other disciplines. Finally, it is time to write, to decide on an interpretation and how to arrange the evidence for readers.

Each book in this series contains an important historical document or group of documents, each document a witness from the past and open to interpretation in different ways. The documents are combined with some element of historical narrative—an introduction or a biographical essay, for example—that provides students with an analysis of the primary source material and important background information about the world in which it was produced.

Each book in the series focuses on a specific topic within a specific historical period. Each provides a basis for lively thought and discussion about several aspects of the topic and the historian's role. Each is short enough (and inexpensive enough) to be a reasonable one-week assignment in a college course. Whether as classroom or personal reading, each book in the series provides firsthand experience of the challenge—and fun—of discovering, recreating, and interpreting the past.

Lynn Hunt
David W. Blight
Bonnie G. Smith
Natalie Zemon Davis
Ernest R. May

Preface

In the summer of 1744 the frontier town of Lancaster, Pennsylvania, sixty miles west of Philadelphia, was the site of a major treaty council between English colonists and Native Americans. Officials from Pennsylvania, Maryland, and Virginia were joined there by 250 Indians, most of them members of the Iroquois (Six Nations) Confederacy from what is now upstate New York. For two weeks, while a crowd of curious locals looked on, colonists and Indians talked, traded jokes, ate and drank together, and even danced together. There was much to talk about, for this was a time of crisis: France and Great Britain had just gone to war again, a clash of empires that was certain to spill over into the two nations' American holdings, and many observers believed that the powerful Iroquois favored the French. After all, the Six Nations and English colonists had quarreled recently about land encroachment, trade abuses, and other contentious issues, squabbles that sometimes ended in bloodshed. Would this council prevent further quarrels and more bloodshed? Could it keep the Iroquois allied to Britain? As it turned out, Lancaster had a happy ending: Both sides went away satisfied, avoiding—at least for the moment—what some considered certain all-out war.

This volume introduces students to what scholars have called one of the most fascinating and most important of the many councils between natives and newcomers in early America. More than that, it invites readers to visit a largely forgotten arena of the colonial experience, a place where peoples from different cultures tried to get along rather than kill one another. Featuring diplomats in place of warriors, words rather than weapons, the treaty minutes provide a useful corrective to common misconceptions about doomed Indians who did nothing more than fight valiantly but hopelessly before disappearing from the American stage. At Lancaster the Iroquois leaders were, to a remarkable degree, running the show, conducting negotiations on *their* terms and not the colonists'.

No less important, the principal document here, the official treaty minutes printed by Benjamin Franklin shortly after the congress closed on July 4, 1744, acquaints students with a genre that has fascinated generations of readers—not only those interested in Native Americans but also students of American history, literature, anthropology, ethnohistory, and linguistics. From whatever direction we approach Franklin's work, the text compels us to consider how well the Iroquois speeches he printed—translated from Iroquois by one colonist, scribbled down in rough notes by another, polished and published by a third—actually convey native voices.

In this volume, Franklin's pamphlet is set amid other material that puts the Lancaster Treaty and minutes in context. The introduction presents the principal players on this diplomatic stage, maps the constellation of problems and opportunities that brought them to Lancaster, sketches Native American diplomatic culture, and attempts to explain the customs that shaped the council, such as handing over large beaded (wampum) belts and punctuating speeches with shouts of "Yo-hah!" or "Huzza!"

The related documents, meanwhile, complicate matters in useful ways by introducing perspectives on the proceedings that raise questions, suggest comparisons, inspire reflection, and promote discussion. One depicts an Indian orator and a colonial secretary during a later treaty, capturing a dramatic moment when different worlds met. This illustration, also featured on the cover of this volume, allows the reader to compare the two councils based on the written descriptions of the Lancaster meeting. Two other texts offer accounts of a vital preliminary council at the Iroquois capital of Onondaga in 1743—one written by a veteran go-between and adopted Iroquois named Conrad Weiser and one by a newcomer to Indian country, the naturalist John Bartram. These contrast with one another in illuminating ways, while also offering a look at how a treaty in an Indian village compared to the one held the next year in a colonial town. Finally, a journal kept by Witham Marshe, a member of the Maryland delegation to the Lancaster Treaty, uncovers what went on behind the scenes, in between the formal speeches chronicled by Benjamin Franklin. Marshe's gossipy tales of drinking and dancing, of wheeling and dealing, bring to life the spectacle of the treaty ground in all its vivid color and gritty texture. Taken together, these accounts of the grand congress at Lancaster in 1744—a volatile mix of summit meeting and circus, of political convention and bazaar—shed light on a shadowy realm that was central to the character of early American life and to the course of early American history.

A number of additional features offer tools for understanding the Lancaster Treaty. The document headnotes provide historical context, and gloss notes explain unfamiliar people and terms. Also included in this volume are a chronology of the Iroquois peoples and their neighbors, questions for consideration to stimulate discussion, and a selected bibliography.

ACKNOWLEDGMENTS

This work originated in two different but intricately and intimately connected places: the archives and libraries where I researched and wrote about the Lancaster council and other Indian treaties for my book *Into the American Woods: Negotiators on the Pennsylvania Frontier*, and the Vassar College classrooms, where, teaching generations of delightfully curious undergraduates about the history of Indians and other Americans, I came to know and appreciate several books in The Bedford Series in History and Culture. In the years since I first thought of making this contribution to that series, both Vassar students and Bedford/St. Martin's editors have continued to help shepherd the work from idea to reality.

At Bedford/St. Martin's, Jane Knetzger and Mary Dougherty were welcoming and encouraging as I got started, Kathryn Abbott gave the manuscript her thorough and thoughtful attention, Laurel Damashek oversaw such complicated matters as permissions and illustrations, and Deborah Prato saved me from many mistakes and missteps. Not least of the publisher's contributions was lining up a tremendously helpful roster of readers for the manuscript. I thank Colin Calloway of Dartmouth College, Ed Gray of Florida State University, Eric Hinderaker of the University of Utah, Dan Mandell of Truman State University (Missouri), Tim Shannon of Gettysburg College, and David Silverman of George Washington University for taking the time and care necessary to suggest ways, large and small, to improve this book.

That the work was in reasonably good shape before it reached those readers and editors is owing to two other sources of assistance. Participants in the Colonial History Workshop at the University of Minnesota spent a sunny summer afternoon indoors with me, giving the introduction a good going over. I am particularly grateful to Eric

Burin, Ed Griffin, John Howe, and Jeani O'Brien for their advice that day and to the University of Minnesota's Department of History for generously providing me office space in the summers I spend in my home state, working on this and other scholarly pursuits.

Finally, a few months before that workshop convened in Minneapolis, I sat down with the Vassar students in my seminar on Native American History—or, as I called them that day, "my guinea pigs"—to hear their thoughts on the entire manuscript. Not content with this lively, wide-ranging, and constructively critical conversation, I also asked (well, *required*) each of them to submit a "reader's report" so I could benefit further from their perspectives as one of the book's intended audiences. My thanks to Matt Bninski, Sarah Boeckmann, Christina Carroll, Federico Delgado, Jen Dixon, Colby Duren, Jenny Gratz, Justin Mahoney, John Palmer, Caitlin Pollock, Liz Prowell, Ian Saxine, Liz Schwartz, Natalie Serkowski, Rob Shatzkin, and Emma Wilk for taking on this task with such gusto and good cheer. They, and their fellow students before and since, have for more than two decades been to me a source of inspiration and enlightenment, of pride and delight. The least I can do in return for all of the Vassar students I have worked with over the years—some now in their forties, some still in their teens—is dedicate this book to them.

James H. Merrell

Contents

Foreword   v

Preface   vii

LIST OF MAPS AND ILLUSTRATIONS   xiii

Major Figures in the Lancaster Treaty of 1744   xiv

PART ONE

**Introduction: Indians and Colonists
in Early America**   **1**

Lancaster, Pennsylvania, June 26, 1744:
An American History Lesson   1
Indians and Other Early Americans   5
The History and Diplomacy of the Iroquois League   10
Treaties between Indians and Colonists   15
The Road to Lancaster   21
The Lancaster Treaty of 1744   25
Treaty Minutes as Historical Texts   27
The Aftermath of the Lancaster Treaty   29

PART TWO
The Document   **39**

A Note about the Text   39

**A Treaty Held at the Town of Lancaster,
in Pennsylvania . . . in June, 1744**   **41**

PART THREE
Related Documents   **89**

1. Benjamin West, *The Indians Giving a Talk to Colonel
    Bouquet . . . in Oct. 1764*, 1766   89
2. John Bartram, *Observations on a Visit to Onondaga*,
    July–August 1743   91
3. Conrad Weiser, *Report on the Council Proceedings at
    Onondaga*, July–August 1743   96
4. Witham Marshe, *Journal of the Treaty Held with the Six
    Nations*, June–July 1744   108

APPENDIXES

A Chronology of the Iroquois Peoples and Their Neighbors
(c. 1300–1830s)   127

Questions for Consideration   131

Selected Bibliography   133

Index   136

Maps and Illustrations

MAPS

1. *Eastern North America in 1744*   2
2. *The Iroquois and Their Neighbors in 1744*   3

ILLUSTRATIONS

1. *Richard Peters*, by John Wollaston[?], c. 1758   6
2. *Benjamin Franklin*, by Robert Feke, c. 1746   7
3. *Wampum Strings*   18
4. *Wampum Belt*   19
5. *A Treaty, Held at the Town of Lancaster, in Pennsylvania* (Title Page)   42

    The Indians Giving a Talk to Colonel Bouquet . . . in Oct. 1764, by Benjamin West, 1766 (Document 1)   90

6. *"The Brave Old Hendrick"*   112

Major Figures
in the Lancaster Treaty of 1744

Many people (and many peoples) appeared on the stage of the Lancaster Treaty negotiations. Those mentioned only once or twice are identified in the footnotes to the texts. Listed here are the lead actors in this drama.

Colonists

Thomas Lee (1690–1750): Head of the Virginia delegation to the Lancaster Treaty, Lee was a member of the Virginia Council of State (the upper house of the assembly).

Richard Peters (1704?–1776): The official scribe at the Lancaster Treaty, Peters was an Anglican clergyman, member of the Pennsylvania Provincial Council, and the Penn family's agent in the province.

George Thomas (c. 1700–1775): Pennsylvania's governor from 1738 to 1747 and the host of the Lancaster Treaty.

Conrad Weiser (1696–1760): The official interpreter at Lancaster, Weiser was a German-born colonist, adopted Iroquois, and go-between for Pennsylvania and the neighboring Indian nations.

Iroquois

Canassatego (1685?–1750): An Onondaga leader who was the chief spokesperson for the Iroquois at Lancaster.

Gachradodon: A Cayuga leader, warrior, and orator.

Shickellamy (?–1748): An Oneida appointed by the Iroquois to oversee relations between the Six Nations and colonists and native peoples in the Susquehanna Valley. He and Conrad Weiser worked together closely from the early 1730s on.

Tocanuntie ("The Black Prince"; ?–1749): An Onondaga who was both a well-known war leader and a diplomat.

Nations of the Iroquois Confederacy

The Iroquois Confederacy was originally composed of five different but related peoples (hence, they were often called "the Five Nations") living in the lands between the Hudson River and the Great Lakes in what is now upstate New York. From east to west, those five nations are as follows:

Mohawks ("the people of the flint")
Oneidas ("the people of the standing stone")
Onondagas ("the people on the mountain")
Cayugas ("the people at the landing")
Senecas ("the people of the great hill")

In about 1722, the Five Nations Iroquois became the Six Nations when they adopted the *Tuscaroras* (a name that might mean "those of the Indian hemp"). These newcomers, who spoke a related Iroquoian language, had migrated from what is now North Carolina after a war with colonists there. Thereafter, colonial writers referred to the Iroquois as both the Five Nations and the Six Nations.

Iroquois Names for Colonies and Colonial Officials

The Iroquois customarily gave names to foreign leaders they dealt with; the name would then be passed on, as a title, to future holders of that position. A term could have different meanings. For example, *Onas* (Pennsylvania) could refer to the colony's founder, William Penn; to the proprietors in 1744 (Penn's sons); to the provincial governor; or to the colony's people more generally.

Assaryquoa ("Sword" or "Big Knife"): Virginia. The term derived from an early Iroquois meeting with that province, when in 1684 Lord Howard of Effingham, Virginia's governor, negotiated with Five Nations leaders at Albany. The Dutch interpreter rendered *Howard* as *Hower* ("cutlass" or "big knife").

Onas ("Feather"): Pennsylvania. This is a play on the name Penn (as in quill, or feather, pen), since *onas* in Iroquois means "feather."

Onontio ("Big Mountain"): Canada. The governor of New France. It derived from the Iroquois name for an early governor of that colony, Charles Huault de Montmagny (*montmagny* translates as "big mountain").

Tocarry-hogan ("Of Two Opinions"): Maryland. Bestowed on Maryland during the 1744 Lancaster Treaty, *Tekarihoken* was the title of the first of the Mohawk sachems who served on the Grand Council of the Iroquois League.

Introduction:
Indians and Colonists
in Early America

LANCASTER, PENNSYLVANIA, JUNE 26, 1744:
AN AMERICAN HISTORY LESSON

One hot summer afternoon in 1744 an Iroquois Indian named Canassatego stood in a county courthouse in the frontier town of Lancaster, Pennsylvania, some sixty miles west of Philadelphia (see Maps 1 and 2). Canassatego was an Onondaga, one of six native nations making up the Iroquois Confederacy (the others were Mohawks, Cayugas, Oneidas, Senecas, and Tuscaroras). A few days earlier, he had walked into Lancaster, leading some 250 other Iroquois—old men and young children, women and warriors—after a long journey south from their villages in what is now upstate New York. They were there to hold talks with officials from the British colonies of Pennsylvania, Maryland, and Virginia, talks aimed at settling disputes over land, making amends for frontier clashes, and strengthening the alliance between the Iroquois and their British-American neighbors.

Besides the Indians and the colonial leaders, scores if not hundreds of curious locals gathered to see the "famous orator" who was "so much admired for his Eloquence." Then about sixty years old, Canassatego was certainly an imposing figure: "a tall, well-made man," remarked one colonist who was there, "very active" and "strong"; above his "very full

1

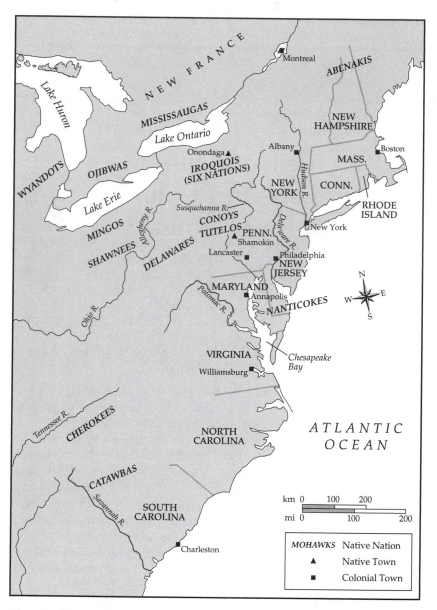

Map 1   *Eastern North America in 1744*

2

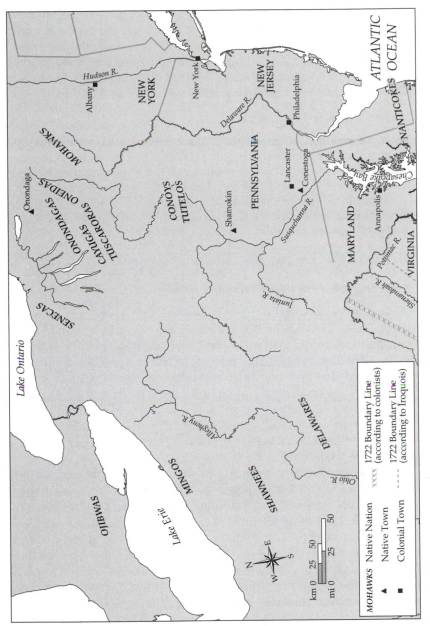

Map 2 *The Iroquois and Their Neighbors in 1744*

chest, and brawny limbs" was "a manly countenance, mixed with a good-natured smile." But he was not smiling now. Pacing back and forth, using a tone of voice more like song than speech, the Iroquois ambassador proceeded to give his audience an American history lesson.[1] The lecture—interpreted by Canassatego's friend, the Pennsylvanian (and adopted Iroquois) Conrad Weiser—began like this:[2]

Brother, the Governor of Maryland,

WHEN you mentioned the Affair of the Land Yesterday, you went back to old Times, and told us, you had been in Possession of the Province of *Maryland* above One Hundred Years; but what is One Hundred Years in Comparison of the Length of Time since our Claim began? since we came out of this Ground? For we must tell you, that long before One Hundred Years our Ancestors came out of this very Ground, and their Children have remained here ever since. You came out of the Ground in a Country that lies beyond the Seas, there you may have a just Claim, but here you must allow us to be your elder Brethren, and the Lands to belong to us long before you knew any thing of them.

Coming upon these words almost two hundred years after Canassatego uttered (and Weiser translated) them, one scholar called the Onondaga's impromptu history tutorial "Indian oratory at its loftiest moment." Another, reading this and other native speeches from the era, concluded that they are "after two hundred years the most original and engaging documents of their century in America." This is quite a claim for a century that produced (among many other texts) Jonathan Edwards's sermon, "Sinners in the Hands of an Angry God," Benjamin Franklin's *Autobiography*, Thomas Jefferson's Declaration of Independence, and Tom Paine's *Common Sense*.[3]

Colonists listening that day in June 1744 were also impressed. They might not have liked *what* Canassatego was saying about being their "elder Brethren" or about their claim to American soil, but they had to admire *how* he and other Iroquois speakers during the treaty said it. Of the Cayuga Gachradodon, who took the floor several days later, Pennsylvania's Governor George Thomas remarked that "he would have made a good figure in the forum of old Rome"—high praise indeed at a time when Englishmen and their colonial cousins were in awe of the ancient Romans. Looking from the remote past to the English present in search of a comparison, one Marylander declared the Cayuga equal to, if not better than, "any of the most celebrated orators he had heard speak."[4]

Even those (like us) not lucky enough to hear Gachradodon or Canassatego in person at Lancaster could enjoy the "virtuoso performance" these Iroquois diplomats put on there. Richard Peters, a Pennsylvania clergyman and provincial official who served as secretary during the council sessions (see Figure 1), predicted that "the Indian treaty will give everyone pleasure that reads it." Back in Philadelphia, Peters handed over the manuscript to his friend, the printer Benjamin Franklin (see Figure 2), who knew well its appeal. "I will send you an Account of it when printed," he promised a London friend in early July, "as the Method of doing Business with those Barbarians may perhaps afford you some Amusement." True to his word, by fall Franklin had published the proceedings (see Part Two) and shipped three hundred copies to England, where leading periodicals like the *Gentleman's Magazine* and *London Magazine* advertised it for sale. Back in America, meanwhile, colonists up and down the coast were so eager to read all about it that he sent copies to New York City and Annapolis, while in Williamsburg, Virginia, another publisher brought out his own edition. Suddenly, little Lancaster—a "filthy" place (one visitor sneered) inhabited by "very great sluts and slovens" along with "an innumerable quantity of bugs, fleas, and vermin"—was the talk of the town on both sides of the Atlantic.[5]

INDIANS AND OTHER EARLY AMERICANS

Famous in Franklin's day, this momentous summit meeting—scholars call it "a pivotal event in the history of the colonies"—is mostly forgotten in our own.[6] Canassatego, Gachradodon, and the rest soon faded into obscurity. Lancaster long ago shed its flea-bitten beginnings to become the capital of "Pennsylvania Dutch Country," a popular tourist attraction. And that 1744 congress is not alone in the neglect it endured. The hundreds of Indian conferences that convened across the continent and across the centuries have suffered a similar fate. Although treaty talk has made its way into the language—*burying the hatchet, clearing the path,* or *kindling a fire* so peace will *last as long as the sun gives light*—the actual conversations that went on, the give-and-take between two worlds that bequeathed to us these evocative metaphors, have faded from memory. If Americans recall any Indian council nowadays, it is likely to be the one a decade after Lancaster at Albany, which again brought hundreds of Six Nations Iroquois face to face with Reverend Peters, Benjamin Franklin, and delegates from

Figure 1   Richard Peters, *by John Wollaston[?], c.1758*

Besides being the Penn family's agent in Pennsylvania, a member of the Provincial Council, and the chief secretary at Lancaster in 1744 and at many other treaties with Indians, Peters was also a minister in the Anglican (Episcopal) Church, the Church of England. He appears here in the garb of a clergyman.

Courtesy of the Pennsylvania Academy of Fine Arts, Philadelphia. Gift of Maria L. M. Peters.

Figure 2 Benjamin Franklin, *by Robert Feke, c. 1746*

Painted around the same time that Franklin published the minutes of the 1744
Lancaster Treaty, Feke's portrait is the first known image of this remarkable
American. The son of a Boston candle and soap maker, Franklin (1706–1790)
started out as a printer's apprentice before running away to Philadelphia in
1723. Two decades later, he had established himself there as the editor and
publisher of *The Pennsylvania Gazette* and *Poor Richard's Almanac*, clerk of
the provincial Assembly, and a leading figure in Philadelphia social, intellec-
tual, and political circles.

several other colonies. Yet, that 1754 conclave is known more as the place Franklin proposed his "Plan of Union" to fellow colonists than as one more link in a long chain of diplomatic encounters between natives and newcomers.[7]

What caused the chronic amnesia about this first incarnation of American foreign policy? One reason might be the *dis*advantage of 20-20 hindsight. Knowing how America's story turned out—with Indian peoples defeated and dispossessed by fraud and by force—it is tempting, even logical, to focus on conquest instead of conversation, on warriors and their battles rather than diplomats and their councils. A second source of forgetfulness could be the habit, when considering Native Americans in past times, of ignoring much of the colonial era. Pocahontas rescuing John Smith, Squanto befriending the Pilgrims— these episodes from the early seventeenth century are an indelible part of American lore. But few can name another episode, or another Indian, from that century—or from the next. Except for an occasional mention of the French and Indian War or Indian Removal, of Tecumseh or Sacajawea, Native Americans tend to show up again on the historical landscape only two hundred years after the English colonies' founding and two thousand miles farther west.

Over the past generation or so, scholars exploring the largely uncharted terrain between Pocahontas and Crazy Horse or Squanto and Sitting Bull have begun to uncover just how much we are missing.[8] Recent work reveals that, in colonial times, Native Americans were more powerful and more pervasive than the conventional story of conquest suggests. Far from leaving the stage after the first act, native peoples continued to play a major role in the American story. For almost two centuries after English folk founded Jamestown and Plymouth, most of the continent remained Indian country: Iroquois, Cherokees, and other nations deployed military might, diplomatic finesse, and economic clout to keep would-be conquerors at bay. As late as 1744, Lancaster—today just an hour's drive from Philadelphia—was near the edge of British colonial settlement.

This new appreciation for a continuing Indian power and an enduring Indian presence makes early America far more complicated—and far more interesting—than previously imagined. A closer look reveals that it was home to a kaleidoscopic array of peoples from Europe, Africa, and America, who mixed and mingled, traded and raided, made war and made love, forged alliances and forged deeds in fascinating fashion. Nor did all of this happen only on the frontier—that permeable, ever-shifting zone between what people at the time referred to as

"English ground" and "the Indian countries."[9] Even late in the colonial era, in neighborhoods long since taken over by colonists, remarkably resilient native groups—Narragansetts in New England, Conestogas near Lancaster, Pamunkeys in Virginia, and Catawbas in Carolina, to name only a few—stubbornly remained as Indian islands in a forbidding sea of strangers. Indeed, it seems as if natives were everywhere in the colonial American realm. They camped out before the "Governor's Palace" in the heart of Williamsburg and peddled brooms or baskets in a wing of the Pennsylvania Statehouse (now known as Independence Hall). They mended stone walls on farms in the Hudson Valley and manned whaleboats on the open sea. They studied at the College of William and Mary and passed off stolen beef as moose meat so the president of Harvard would buy it. They were woodworkers in Virginia and potters in Carolina, preachers in New England and "Indian Attornies" in New Jersey.[10]

Never was the natives' visibility more vividly recorded than in the summer of 1744, the very season of the Lancaster Treaty. As the Iroquois delegation and its colonial counterparts converged on that frontier town, a Scottish physician named Alexander Hamilton (no relation to the Founding Father) set out from his new home in Annapolis, heading north. Unlike the Maryland treaty commissioners—many of them his friends—the doctor was bound not for Lancaster but for Philadelphia, New York, Boston, and other points along the coast road, with a side trip up the Hudson River to Albany. And unlike his fellow travelers, Hamilton was not negotiating; he was sightseeing—and seeking cooler, drier air that might help fight the tuberculosis that plagued him.

The lively journal that the Scotsman kept on his trip reveals that he regularly bumped into native peoples of all sorts. Riding through Princeton, Hamilton received the customary Delaware greeting, "How' s't ni tap," from "an Indian traveller." Along the Rhode Island coast, the sojourner dropped in on a headman who "lives after the English mode": His wife wore "a high modish dress in her silks, hoops, stays, and dresses like an English woman"; he treated guests to a glass of fine wine, and he struck even the snobbish Hamilton as "a very . . . mannerly man." Nearby the doctor came upon "naked" Indians— "wretches" who were "lazy" and "indolent," the traveler sniffed—collecting oysters for breakfast. Farther up the road in Boston, the visitor went to church and saw natives sitting in a nearby pew. Two days later, he gawked at a diplomatic delegation from Indian country striding down a main thoroughfare. These and the other casual encounters

Dr. Hamilton recorded show that, even as delegates from three provinces and ten nations assembled in Lancaster, native threads could be found throughout the fabric of everyday colonial life.[11]

County courtroom and college classroom, Indian town and Boston church, frontier battlefield and urban market—of all the places where natives and newcomers crossed paths, few were more colorful, or more crucial to shaping the course of events, than the council ground. The throngs of Pennsylvanians that followed Canassatego and his people into Lancaster in June 1744—like the hordes who listened to his speech a few days later, the swarms that returned to the courthouse just "to see the Indians dine," and the tourists who in the evening dropped by the Iroquois camp on the outskirts of town—were entranced by these exotic visitors, by their dances and drums, their painted faces and enchanting children.[12] No doubt the Indian visitors were also curious about the strange new world that these people from (as Canassatego put it) "a Country that lies beyond the Seas" were building on the borders of Iroquois territory.

But Lancaster was much more than mere spectacle or entertainment. Like all treaties, it was "compelling theater, a lively stage on which the peoples of early America acted out the contest for the continent." At that town in 1744 and at scores of other congresses, those whom Indians termed "Great Ones" or "old and wise people" would get together to talk about *Caligh Wanorum* (Iroquois for "matters of great consequence"). It was here that natives and colonists tried to clear what historian Richard White calls a "middle ground" between peoples who spoke different languages, wore different clothes, and worshipped different gods. It was here that they looked for a meeting of minds on vital issues like trade and territory, war and peace. It is not claiming too much to say that Lancaster and other councils were matters of life and death, that they helped shape the fate of nations, indeed of America itself. For their ringing oratory, their human drama, and their historical importance, they deserve our attention.[13]

THE HISTORY AND DIPLOMACY OF THE IROQUOIS LEAGUE

Long before Canassatego rose to speak in the Lancaster courthouse that June day in 1744, Iroquois peoples had made themselves masters of the art of diplomacy. The origins of their skill can be traced back to the founding of the Iroquois League itself. Unlike the United States—

which celebrates its July 4, 1776, birthday every year—the League's beginnings are impossible to date precisely. In part this is due to a lack of records, in part it is because the Iroquois peoples probably came together gradually. Their union was "not a single event," historian Daniel K. Richter suggests, "but a series of alliances negotiated over a long period."[14] Some say those negotiations might have gotten under way a generation or two before Christopher Columbus sailed west; others believe it was more like a century or two before. But all agree that at some point peoples in the lands between the Hudson River and the Great Lakes, towns and tribes speaking similar languages and leading similar lives, stopped attacking each other and began talking to each other. Up to that time, Iroquois tradition has it, "everywhere there was peril and everywhere mourning"; the country later called *Iroquoia*—the lands stretching west from the Hudson—was infested by "feuds with outer nations, feuds with brother nations, feuds of sister towns and feuds of families and clans."[15]

Into this toxic atmosphere of bloodshed and grief, as Iroquois tell it, came a godlike being named Deganawidah bearing words of peace and ceremonies designed to dry tears, heal broken hearts, and promote reconciliation. Traveling from one town and one nation to the next with his disciple, an Onondaga named Hiawatha, he helped turn people's thoughts away from death and destruction. The formula for this cure was special incantations bearing the power to calm minds and ease sorrow, reinforced by tangible objects such as shell beads (wampum) on strings or belts that gave words weight and helped "lift away the darkness." From that sojourn emerged the Great League of Peace among five nations—Mohawks, Cayugas, Oneidas, Onondagas, and Senecas (the sixth nation, Tuscaroras, would join a generation or so before the Lancaster Treaty)—with its capital, or "council fire," at Hiawatha's town of Onondaga (modern Syracuse). There, fifty leaders (*sachems*)—"men of sense" from each group, selected by the older women—would gather for meetings of the "Grand Council." There, reported a French observer in 1668, "they hold every year a general assembly. There all the Deputies from the different Nations are present, to make their complaints and receive the necessary satisfaction in mutual gifts,—by means of which they maintain a good understanding with one another."[16]

Part of that understanding was that their real name—not *Iroquois* (a term of uncertain origin given to them by others) but *Haudenosaunee* ("People of the Longhouse")—literally and figuratively captured this developing sense of community.[17] Whether Cayuga or

Oneida, Mohawk or Seneca, Haudenosaunee lived in bark-covered houses, twenty-five feet wide and eighty or more feet long; in each glowed several fires, around which clustered several families. But to the natives' way of thinking, the League itself was a Longhouse, too, consisting of five "fires," or nations, with Mohawks guarding the "Eastern Door" near the Hudson and Senecas as sentinels of the "Western Door" (see Map 2 on p. 3).

Regularly retelling the story of Deganawidah and Hiawatha, of the League and the "Great Peace" it embodied, the Five Nations, before seeing their first European, had forged a sense of a common heritage and a shared destiny. Despite what those first Europeans thought, however, this entity bore little resemblance to a central government. The Grand Council at Onondaga was more spiritual than political, more a matter of sustaining "good thoughts" and "good understanding" among peoples than of hammering out domestic or foreign policy. Each nation—indeed, each village, even each kin group—was free to chart its own course, a course set by men and women alike, meeting separately to discuss public affairs. As one colonist wrote, Iroquois women "hold their councils apart and, as a result of their decisions, advise the chiefs." Thus advised, even instructed, Iroquois leaders could persuade or cajole, but they could not command.[18]

Thus, the League offered its members both a sense of unity—and of power and prestige derived from that unity—as well as a certain independence in conducting their own affairs. This flexible union, combined with a strategic position astride major highways running east-west (from the Hudson River to the Great Lakes) and north-south (through the Hudson, Delaware, Susquehanna, and Allegheny river valleys), made the Haudenosaunee a force to be reckoned with.

Is all this just ancient history? Hardly. The beginning of what Gachradodon at Lancaster called "the united Nations" was perhaps even more vivid and more relevant to his people in 1744 than America's founding is to us today. At the opening session of a council in Onondaga the summer before Lancaster—a gathering summoned to pave the way for those talks—Canassatego and Conrad Weiser had listened as an Iroquois speaker, following custom, once more "rehearsed the beginning of the Union of the five Nations, Praised their Grandfathers' Wisdom in establishing the Union or Alliance, by which they became a formidable Body; that they (now living) were but Fools to their wise Fathers, Yet protected and accompanied by their Fathers' Spirit."[19] As Canassatego and his fellow Iroquois knew, the League was the direct ancestor of the Lancaster Treaty. The proceedings in that frontier courthouse in 1744 would have been familiar to a Mohawk or an Oneida living in 1644 or 1544. The very tools and values that Iroquois fashioned to construct connections between neighbors in a longhouse or a town, then between towns and among the Iroquois nations, were used to create new entities in the years between the League's founding and Lancaster.[20]

One of those new entities was the Iroquois *Confederacy*, a related and complementary body more concerned with politics and foreign policy, which began to take shape a century or so before Canassatego's day in response to the perils (such as devastating diseases and land encroachment) and possibilities (such as trade) brought on by European colonization. The Confederacy, often confused with the League by colonists then and scholars since, did indeed overlap with the older Iroquois League in some ways: It met at Onondaga, it employed similar rituals, and it even included a few of the same men who were League sachems on the Grand Council. But the Confederacy was a political and diplomatic forum, not the fountain of "Iroquois culture and spiritual unity" that the League was. Moreover, the Confederacy's public face was not the League Sachems (none of whom apparently attended the Lancaster Treaty) but, rather, men made prominent by their renown as warriors, diplomats, and orators—men like Canassatego.[21]

Inspired and equipped by League traditions, during the seventeenth century the Iroquois Confederacy began to expand its reach, to extend "the Great Tree of Peace" that Deganawidah and Hiawatha had planted at Onondaga and that already sheltered the Five Nations. War parties ranged far and wide to capture foes—the Five Nations were neither the first nor the last to make war in the name of peace—and bring them home, often adopting them and making them members of clans and towns. Statesmen, meanwhile, worked on a larger scale, employing the combination of warm words and cold threats you will overhear at Lancaster (see Part Two) to get smaller native groups— Nanticokes and Conoys from Maryland, Tutelos and Saponis from Virginia, Tuscaroras from Carolina—to move north and become allies and tributaries—or, as the Iroquois termed them, "props" of the Longhouse. (Tuscaroras actually became a sixth nation, a junior partner in the Confederacy.) It was this potent combination of warriors harassing other Indian nations and ambassadors wooing those same nations that enabled the Iroquois to claim, by right of conquest, ownership of the lands in Maryland and Virginia that Canassatego asserted at Lancaster in 1744.

With the arrival of the Dutch, English, and French on the borders of Iroquois Country beginning in the early seventeenth century, the Five Nations sought to embrace the newcomers in similar fashion.[22] Treating with (and sometimes fighting with) New France and New Netherland, with New England and (after the English conquest of Dutch New Netherland in 1664) New York, Iroquois foreign policy enabled them to acquire new, powerful friends and new, powerful goods such as muskets, axes, hoes, and cloth. Strategically situated between English and French empires that, throughout the colonial era, were locked in fierce competition—and sometimes open warfare—for eastern North America, the Iroquois made the most of it by playing one European power against the other, promising friendship to both while tying themselves to neither. Never was this balancing act more evident than in 1701, when—in gatherings convened at Onondaga, Albany, and Montreal—the Five Nations negotiated several major treaties with New York and New France simultaneously, agreements that made them friends of both these bitter foes. Half a century later, the Iroquois adroitly kept that precarious perch between empires. "To preserve the Ballance between us & the French," noted one English colonist in 1750, "is the great ruling Principle of the Modern Indian Politics."[23]

Iroquois emissaries sought similar advantages—and worked similar magic—by negotiating with several British provinces simultaneously. The centerpiece of the Five Nations' ties with these provinces was "the Covenant Chain," a series of alliances forged first with New York in the late 1670s and then expanded to include other native nations and additional English colonies.[24] As provincial officials at Lancaster in 1744 recalled, envoys from Maryland and Virginia had visited Albany before 1680 to hold their first talks with Iroquois ambassadors. In 1701, while most Five Nations diplomats were occupied with New France and New York, a solitary Onondaga named Ahookasoongh was in Philadelphia to make his people's first overtures to the new colony of Pennsylvania, founded by the Quaker leader William Penn two decades before. To the consternation of New York officials and New York merchants who wanted Iroquois allies and customers for themselves, between Ahookasoongh's visit in 1701 and Canassatego's in 1744 lay a series of conferences that, as natives would say, "cleared the path" between Iroquoia and Pennsylvania and "kindled a council fire" where formal talks could take place. Given this history of Iroquois diplomatic strategy, it should be no surprise that in the summer of 1744, while Canassatego and his comrades were at

Lancaster, another Iroquois delegation traveled to Boston to meet with Massachusetts officials (the Indians Dr. Alexander Hamilton saw on the street that day were Mohawks), while a third party visited Albany to renew the New York alliance. For the Six Nations, this three-pronged approach was diplomatic business as usual.[25]

By then, Iroquois skill in dealing with Pennsylvanians for a generation and with European colonists for a century had made the Six Nations, as Canassatego told the courthouse crowd at the close of the Lancaster Treaty on July 4, a "formidable" and "powerful Confederacy." To be sure, these were troubled times in Iroquoia: Famine and disease stalked the land, the French and the English were crowding in, unprecedented amounts of liquor brought by colonial traders flooded the villages and befuddled the people, and the leaders were often divided on important issues.[26]

Nonetheless, so adept were the Six Nations at navigating these treacherous waters that few colonists would have disputed Canassatego's July 4 claim. Earlier in the proceedings Governor Thomas, urging his colleagues from Virginia and Maryland to help in "cultivating a good Understanding with them," had reminded the commissioners of "the Importance of these Nations to us": As friends, they "are capable of defending their [colonial] Settlements," as foes, "of making cruel Ravages upon" those settlements. "If we lose the Iroquois," fretted another Pennsylvania official, "we are gone."[27] Hard as it might be to believe, a confederacy with a population of less than 10,000 (at a time when Britain's thirteen mainland colonies approached one million) seemed to hold the fate of the continent in its hands. No wonder, as one colonist put it in 1741, Iroquois "seem always to have Lookd upon themselves as far Superiour to the Rest of Mankind and accordingly Call themselves *Ongwehoenwe*, i.e., Men Surpassing all other men."[28]

TREATIES BETWEEN INDIANS AND COLONISTS

Feared and courted, at Lancaster (as at other councils during the colonial era) the Six Nations were, to a degree, able to write the script and run the show. Iroquois control over the proceedings was evident even before the talks got under way, for they had final say over where and when the conference would convene. Virginians wanted Williamsburg and Marylanders proposed Annapolis, but their counterparts at Onondaga were having none of that. Nor would they follow a schedule set by colonists, insisting instead on late spring, since that was the best time for peeling the elm bark needed to make the canoes that would take them most of the way from Iroquoia to Lancaster.[29]

Once everyone finally assembled in June, the talks unfolded largely "according to the Indian Custom."[30] Strict attention to "Custom" was necessary because, to natives, the essence of friendship between peoples lay not in what the colonists thought of as the end *product*— the published proceedings—but in the entire *process* of negotiation. Shared meals and quiet chats "in the bushes" away from the light of the "Council Fire" were, to Indians, every bit as important for conjuring the proper harmonious atmosphere as grand orations during public sessions. Because peace, to them, was a feeling, not a document, it demanded the cultivation of "good thoughts"—and that, in turn, meant that things had to be done a certain way.[31]

The very pace of the treaty followed the Iroquois habit of going slowly. Rather than plunging right in as soon as they reached town, natives took several days to pitch camp, recover from the journey, and hold preliminary talks among themselves and with colonists. Even after the public proceedings commenced, this unhurried tempo prevailed. Because, as one Iroquois later put it, "Publick Business required great Consideration," no speech ought to be answered at once. Preparing a proper reply entailed careful deliberation among the native envoys to reach a consensus. "There is nothing they contemn so much as precipitation [haste] in publick councils," remarked a Pennsylvanian in 1743, "and they consequently spin out a Treaty . . . to a great length of time."[32]

The formal speeches colonists delivered also bore an Indian imprint, for provincial leaders heeded the advice Conrad Weiser gave at an earlier council: that the Six Nations must be "spoke to in their own way."[33] This meant, for one thing, that the conversation would be conducted in Iroquois, even though some natives knew English. For another, it meant that colonists would borrow the rich metaphorical rhetoric that was a central feature of Indian oratory. In that vocabulary, concrete objects (paths and hatchets, chains and fires), parts of the body (ears and eyes, hands and heart), or kin connections (cousins and brothers, fathers and children) conveyed abstract ideas of war or peace, friendship or enmity. Hence, when Pennsylvania's Governor George Thomas (coached by Weiser) made his first speech to the Iroquois on June 25, he began with talk of "Brethren" who had "come to enlarge the Fire, which was almost gone out, and to make it burn clearer; to brighten the Chain which had contracted some Rust, and to renew their Friendship with you," a friendship that should "last so long as the Sun, the Moon and the Stars, shall give Light."[34]

That Thomas said these words while holding a belt woven of wampum shell beads and then laid it on a table "to enforce what had been said" further attests to how far a British official would go to respect Iroquois values. Ever since the days of Hiawatha and Deganawidah, strings and belts of beads fashioned from a type of seashell found on Long Island Sound had been indispensable to talks between peoples (see Figures 3 and 4 on pp. 18–19). "Without Wampum," noted one colonist, "Nothing is to be done Amongst the Indians" because, as an Iroquois said, the beads helped a speaker's words "have Credit with" his audience. In part this was because the difficulty of finding and stringing shells required many hands (especially women's hands), thereby attesting to the fact that an orator was speaking for many, whether a town, a nation, or a confederacy. An added advantage of wampum was that its pattern of dark and light beads could serve as a reminder of a particular topic or agreement, both for the man delivering the speech (and the wampum) at a treaty and, even years later, for those who received and preserved the strings and belts, often in an official "Counsel Bagg."[35]

Hauling out beaded strings or belts, mouthing jargon about "fires" or "paths," waiting and waiting for an answer to a speech—colonists often chafed at the constraints imposed by Indian diplomatic rules. The pace seemed glacial, the speeches endless and tedious. "I fear," wrote Virginia Governor William Gooch to that colony's delegation on the eve of the treaty, that this affair "will give you an unexpected occasion for the Exercise of your Patience, and that calmness of mind so absolutely necessary to enable you to bear those solemn Wranglings and Brawlings you must submit to, in debating the important Points of your Embassy." But once again Weiser reminded impatient provincial officials that what might seem "only Ceremonies and meer triffling to an European Idea" were in fact key variables in the diplomatic equation, for "the Indians always observe Such things."[36]

Happily or not, colonists went along because they had to: The Iroquois Confederacy's strategic location and its reputation as a military power demanded nothing less. But it helped that, foreign as Indian diplomacy seemed, it was not wholly at odds with "an European Idea" of such matters. As historian Nancy Shoemaker has observed, beneath the obvious differences between natives and newcomers "rested a bedrock of shared ideas" about nations and territories, peace and

Figure 3 *Wampum Strings*

Before Europeans arrived in America, native peoples made cylindrical beads by drilling holes in a species of seashells (from the Algonquian word *wampumpeag*) that were found most abundantly on Long Island Sound. Colonists considered these objects "Indian money," but in fact their value was spiritual and symbolic. Strung together (usually by Indian women), they could be worn as a visible sign of status or, in diplomacy, carried and displayed as proof of an ambassador's authority. During treaties, strings such as these were also used for less important passages of an envoy's message. They would be held by the speaker, then handed over to mark the end of one portion of an oration. Europeans soon began producing and trading glass beads, and Native Americans sometimes substituted them for wampum, but the powerful significance of beads on strings remained.

The University of Pennsylvania Museum (image #142742).

war, and much more besides.[37] Both peoples considered treaties a good way of doing business. Both admired eloquent orators. Both thought that what might seem like incidentals cluttering up Lancaster's main event—sharing a meal or a smoke, toasting one another's good health—helped foster friendship. Both even had a habit of loudly registering agreement with what was being said: The Iroquois shout "Yo-hah!" bore some resemblance to colonists' "Huzza!"[38] In fact, while the Six Nations seem to be in charge of the proceedings—setting the date, controlling the pace, dictating forms if not terms—the treaty text also reveals how far English ways played a powerful role in shaping the course of events. Some scholars have termed the minutes Richard Peters took down and Benjamin Franklin printed up (Part Two) "hybrid Iroquois-European creations."[39]

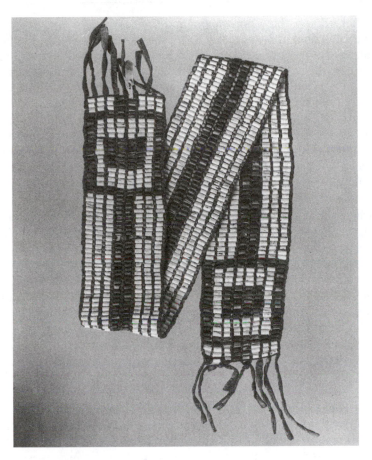

Figure 4 *Wampum Belt*

As at Lancaster in 1744, important parts of a message would be punctuated not by wampum strings alone but by strings woven together to form a belt. Though colonists failed to appreciate the significance of it, native women ordinarily were the weavers, for that task signified their assent to the words contained in the belt. Many belts had patterns designed to signify the contents and aid in remembering their meaning. Natives, keeping these belts in a "council bag," regularly met to pull out these objects and refresh the people's memories of the agreements. Colonists were astonished that an Indian who had been properly educated about the meaning of a particular belt could, many years later, read it and repeat the substance of an agreement. This Iroquois belt is of unknown date, origin, and meaning, but it might depict an alliance (the row of dark beads running its length) between two peoples (the squares at either end).

The University of Pennsylvania Museum (image #12972).

It helped, too, that Canassatego and Conrad Weiser were present to play up the similarities and play down the differences. Of all the ingredients in the recipe for a successful council, perhaps none was more important than having men conversant with both cultures, men the Iroquois termed "fitt & proper Persons to goe between the Six Nations & [colonial governments]." These two go-betweens might seem an odd couple: One was a respected Onondaga leader, the other was a middle-aged German farmer, local magistrate, and sometime religious mystic who lived thirty miles from Lancaster. But the course of Weiser's life had brought him into the Iroquois orbit at an early age, and he never escaped entirely. Arriving in America as a teenager in 1710 to settle with his family on the New York frontier, he lived among nearby Mohawks for a time (his father, struggling to get land and food, was happy to have one less mouth to feed and hoped for an interpreter he could trust). Then in the late 1720s Conrad moved with his wife and young family to the Pennsylvania borderlands. There his Iroquois connections brought him to the attention of Philadelphia officials keen to forge closer ties with the Six Nations. By 1736 Iroquois leaders were announcing delightedly "that they had found Conrad faithfull and honest; that he is a true good Man, & had spoke their [colonists'] Words & our Words, and not his own."[40]

Six years later it was Canassatego who sang Weiser's praises. Friendship requires "a Skillful and honest Person to go between Us, one in whom both You and We can place a Confidence," he informed Pennsylvania officials at a July 1742 treaty in Philadelphia. "We esteem our present Interpreter to be such a person, equally faithful in the Interpretation of what ever is said to him by either of Us, equally allied to both, He is of our Nation and a Member of our Council as well as of Yours. When we adopted him we divided him into two equal Parts, one we kept for our selves and one we left for You." Weiser felt the same way about his Onondaga counterpart, describing Canassatego to Governor Thomas as "our Particular Friend and well acquainted both with Indians & white People's Affairs & Customs."[41]

So confident was Thomas in Weiser (aided by Canassatego) that in January 1744, as plans for Lancaster moved forward, he hired the German on behalf of Virginia and Maryland without even asking permission from his counterparts in Annapolis and Williamsburg. "It is my opinion," he wrote Governor Gooch after the fact, "that neither your Government nor that of Maryland will be able to carry on the Treaty without him." Thomas was right: The upcoming congress desperately needed accomplished go-betweens. Whether even Weiser and Canassatego would be enough, however, was another matter. They would need all their skills—and a little luck—to pull off a successful treaty, for it was, everyone agreed, a "Critical & Dangerous time" when the frontier was "overshadow'd . . . by a very dark Cloud."[42]

THE ROAD TO LANCASTER

The crisis that both required and imperiled the 1744 Lancaster Treaty emerged from a volatile combination of long-standing grievances and recent clashes that pushed Indians and their British neighbors to the brink of all-out war. Natives had been complaining for years about trade with colonists, accusing them of inflating prices or of giving an Indian free rum and cheating him while he was intoxicated. Colonists, meanwhile, objected to the way native travelers—traders en route to market, warriors on the trail of their foes—sometimes helped themselves to a farmer's corn or cattle when they needed a meal. Those natives, accustomed to hospitality from the locals whenever they traversed Indian country, considered colonists stingy and the food their just due, whereas the colonists labeled the Indians thieves.[43]

The sorest point, however, was land. Native anger about crooked sales engineered by colonists and about squatters sneaking onto Indian territory went back two generations, and the situation was getting worse, not better. For one thing, Pennsylvania's population exploded in this era—climbing from about 18,000 people in 1700 to some 86,000 four decades later—and these newcomers were eager to buy tracts from the current proprietors (owners) of the province: founder William Penn's sons, Richard, John, and Thomas. For another, those three lacked their father's habit of treating Indians fairly. In 1737 the Penns used a fake deed, a false map, and a genuine threat to carry out the infamous "Walking Purchase" of Delaware territory above Philadelphia. Brandishing a supposed 1686 agreement that a land sale's boundaries would be set by how far a man can *walk* in a day and a half, the proprietors and their agents took that and, well, *ran* with it, sending runners tearing along a cleared path that cut cross-country rather than sauntering beside the river's meandering course, as Indians had expected. As a result, the Penns acquired a domain roughly the size of Rhode Island, set about removing its Delaware owners, and ignored Indian objections that this "Running Walk" was "Fraud and great Fraud." Yet, Thomas Penn, the lead proprietor, was still not satisfied: The man "keeps begging & plagueing us to Give Him some [more] Land . . . ," Delawares complained in 1740. "He Wearies us Out of Our Lives." Not only that, they added two months later, but when they tried to live on their land in peace and "Enjoy our Birth Rights . . . we Are abused [by colonial settlers] as if We Were Enemies & not Friends" and were "in danger of being Cut to peices [sic] & destroyed So that," they added ominously, "We Cannot keep our Young People in Ord[e]r."[44]

The Iroquois had a hand in this shady business, backing their Pennsylvania allies instead of their Delaware "cousins." At a 1742 treaty in Philadelphia, Canassatego himself publicly rebuked Delaware leaders for continuing to protest the Walking Purchase: "You ought to be taken by the Hair of the Head and shak'd severely till you recover your Senses . . . ," he scolded. "You don't know what . . . you are doing. Our Brother Onas' Case is very just and plain . . . ; on the other Hand your Cause is bad, your Heart far from being upright. . . . We charge You to remove instantly." Yet, just a few days earlier, Canassatego had fretted to his "Brother Onas" that the Six Nations might be the next to lose their domain. Colonists had not paid a fair price for previous purchases, he said, nor have they respected the new boundaries created by those agreements. "Your People daily settle on these Lands [still owned by the Six Nations] and spoil our Hunting. We must insist on your removing them." Not only that, but the merchandise the province had handed over for territory the Iroquois sold in 1736 was "extremely little. . . . We know our Lands are now become more Valuable; the white People think we don't know their Value, but we are sensible that the Land is Everlasting, and the few Goods we receive for it are soon Worn out and Gone."[45]

Further imperiling friendship was the Iroquois claim to territories that were now part of Virginia and Maryland. This, a central point of contention at Lancaster in 1744, had its origins at another council with Pennsylvania eight years earlier. There, Six Nations leaders surrendered lands on the lower Susquehanna River. In return, these emissaries won from the province a pledge to help them get payment from Maryland and Virginia for lands the Iroquois said they owned because they had conquered native peoples living there. Some modern scholars question these claims to territory where no Iroquois had ever resided and these alleged conquests of shadowy groups. One historian bluntly calls such talk "bogus."[46] Certainly Pennsylvania authorities at that 1736 treaty session were puzzled: "We do not clearly understand this Matter . . . ," they replied; "we know not how this is supported."

Their fellow colonists to the south were more than puzzled—they were outraged, insisting that such assertions were fraudulent and should be ignored. After waiting six years for a reply, it was the Six Nations' turn to be angry. "We have never heard from you [about this matter]," Canassatego scolded Governor Thomas during the 1742 Philadelphia treaty, then insisted that Thomas contact "the Person whose people are seated on our Lands [to the south and] press him to send Us a positive Answer; Let him say Yes or No [about paying the Iroquois]." The Onondaga warned darkly, "If No, we are able to do ourselves Justice, and we will do it by going to take payment . . . ourselves."[47]

Even as Canassatego was issuing veiled threats that summer, in Maryland the governor was calling out the militia and ordering that Nanticokes—natives living amid colonists on Maryland's Eastern Shore who were also "props" in the Iroquois Longhouse (that is, part of the Confederacy)—be disarmed and imprisoned. Rumor had it that unnamed "Northern Indians"—some said Shawnees, some Six Nations, some both—had convinced Nanticokes to join them "to rise and cut off the English."[48] That threat soon subsided, but by year's end idle talk spilled over into actual bloodshed when an Iroquois war party, heading south to fight their Catawba foes, passed through the Shenandoah Valley on Virginia's frontier and got into a skirmish with the locals. The clash, which left eight colonists and four Iroquois dead, sent the survivors scurrying off to spread the alarm throughout colonial territory and Indian country. In no time, anxious natives gathered in their towns for safety, while terrified colonists in Pennsylvania and elsewhere—convinced "that the Indians . . . were come to a Resolution to cut off all the white People"—abandoned their farms and fled the frontier. "I hoped," sighed Governor Thomas, writing to Conrad Weiser when the grim news reached the Pennsylvania capital, "that our last Treaty with the six Nations [in Philadelphia during the summer of 1742] would have made Us easy for some Time to come as to all Indian Affairs, but . . . if things are not prudently managed, [war seems certain]."[49]

Fortunately for Thomas and everyone else, Weiser was able to "prevent the Flame spreading wider" by going to Onondaga that summer, in Virginia's name, to placate the Iroquois and convince them to visit Lancaster the next year so the two sides could formally "bury the hatchet" and "dispell the Dark Cloud that overshadowed Us for some Time, that the Sun may shine again."[50]

Between Onondaga in 1743 and Lancaster in 1744, however, lurked still more trouble. One February morning, somewhere in the snowy wastes west of the Susquehanna River, Delaware Indians brutally murdered three Pennsylvania fur traders in a spat over a debt. This "very unhappy Affair," as one native later called it, was "something worse than any thing that ever happened before" between William Penn's people and their native neighbors. "A great noise arose" among the Indians, for they were "a feared there would be Some Blood Shed about it before all was over." Meanwhile, furious frontier folk demanded that natives surrender the suspects, adding ominously that "we do not want to fall out or quarrel with you without [unless] you make us do it." Once again a weary Weiser set out for Indian country to stave off war.[51]

As the go-between met with Indians in early May to quiet the noise, even worse news was making its way to Philadelphia: After three decades of a fragile peace, France and England were again at war.[52] This was not exactly a surprise. In July 1742 Governor Thomas, even then "in Daily Expectation of a French War," had nervously asked Canassatego, "I suppose if the French should go to Warr with Us you'l join them"? The Onondaga's reply—"We shall always be faithful and True to you, our Old and good Allies"—was reassuring, but no amount of talk could allay fears. Rumor had it that not only did Delawares and Shawnees favor France, but the Six Nations did, too. Imperial war and bitter land disputes, vicious rumors and equally vicious killings—considering the items on the Lancaster agenda, it is no wonder that more than one scholar has called this council "not only one of the most interesting but also one of the most crucial of all the treaties."[53]

At this perilous time, it did not help that some of what Virginia Governor William Gooch had called "Wranglings and Brawlings" took place not just between Indians and colonists but among England's various provinces. New Yorkers, long fancying themselves the Six Nations' closest colonial friends, resented Pennsylvania's campaign to claim that title by hosting the treaty and mediating between the Iroquois and the southern colonies. The Maryland men also had little love for Penn's people. Having fought their neighbor to the north over the location of their shared boundary line, Annapolis officials were convinced that Philadelphia men were now using the Six Nations to make life difficult. "The Indians had no thoughts of making any demands for lands in this Province," one Marylander grumbled, until meddling Pennsylvanians "infused a notion into their heads that they had some pretensions." Equally suspicious of Weiser, they "infected" Virginia treaty commissioners (who stopped in Annapolis en route to

Lancaster) with the same mistrust. Working together, the two colonies secretly contacted New York in an effort to line up a different go-between and to get a second opinion on the validity of Iroquois claims. By the time Colonel Thomas Lee and the rest of the Virginia delegation reached Philadelphia in late May for preliminary talks with officials there, it was obvious that they were not feeling very diplomatic. A disgusted Richard Peters wrote that, speaking of "the Indians with great Contempt, . . . the Comm[issione]rs. of Virginia were of Opinion, the Indians had no Claim on them for any Lands[,] they were determin'd to bear it with an high Hand and try if they cou'd not frigthen [sic] the Indians into a renunciation of their Claims on Virginia."[54]

This "haughty overbearing Virginian" Lee is "as full of . . . Chicanery [trickery] as an Attorney," one Pennsylvania official lamented. What Peters called the "seven flaming fine Gentlemen" the treaty commissioner brought along from Williamsburg were no better. Having met them and given them "full Scope to vent all they had on their Minds," the Pennsylvania councilor and clergyman was pessimistic about what Lancaster might accomplish. "I wish the ensuing treaty may end well," he confided to Proprietor Thomas Penn, then in England, "but I very much doubt it, being afraid of the narrowness and haughtiness of the Virginians and Marylanders, which, added to their unacquaintedness with Indian affairs, make but a poor prospect [of success]."[55]

THE LANCASTER TREATY OF 1744

As the time for the treaty congress approached, Peters and others immersed in preparations had plenty of other reasons to doubt—and even to despair. Anyone who has ever had to arrange a meeting can sympathize with those handling this dreary task in 1744. Imagine the logistical nightmare of assembling at the same time and place several hundred people from three different English colonies and ten different Indian nations—especially without snail mail, e-mail, phones, or faxes. Even figuring out when the Indian delegation might show up was a guessing game at best. At Onondaga on July 31, 1743, the headmen told Weiser that "we will set out [for the treaty] from our several Towns after eight Moons are past by, when the ninth just is to be seen, this present Moon, which is almost expired, not to be reckoned."[56] If that sounds confusing, it was—at least to the colonists. Unaccustomed to counting moons, they guessed that this meant May;

when May came and went with no sign of Indians, officials waiting in Philadelphia suffered "great anxiety" and became "very impatient at so unreasonable and so unexpected a Detention." Were Canassatego and company coming at all? Had they indeed joined the French foe?[57]

When the delegation finally arrived on Pennsylvania's borders (following the Iroquois schedule), Peters and his colleagues in the capital heaved a sigh of relief. Conrad Weiser's worries, on the other hand, were just beginning. The guests—all 245 of them by his count—were hot, tired, thirsty, and hungry when he first shook hands with them at a fur trader's house beside the Susquehanna River on June 15. The week it took him to escort this crowd the last sixty miles to Lancaster was filled with fretting. The go-between hired wagons to carry the lame and dispatched messengers to alert the authorities. He got millers to part with bushel upon bushel of flour, arranged for sheep and steers to be butchered, and bought enough beer and rum to wash it all down. Once at the treaty site, Weiser stayed busy keeping the Indians happy: He paid a blacksmith to mend their weapons, bought two hats for an Oneida named Onicknayqua and gave two tobacco boxes to Canassatego, found a blanket for this person and a jacket for that one. Lancaster locals watching Weiser scurry about had their own troubles, for the gentlemen from three colonial capitals who descended on the town en masse were accustomed to the finest food and lodging, both of which were in short supply. Not only did the hinterlands offer "sorry rum" and "nauseous eggs and bacon," but the beds were infested with bugs and the "very bad" water caused diarrhea. As if that were not enough to provoke a proper gentleman, there were few barbers—and no backgammon tables at all![58]

Bringing together British colonial officials who were famous for their haughtiness and Indians who called themselves *Ongwehoenwe* ("Men Surpassing all other men") at a location neither liked and then expecting them to converse civilly about unpleasant subjects like who fired first and whose land claims were fraudulent was a recipe for trouble—and trouble soon arrived. Weiser had to warn the younger "flaming fine Gentlemen" touring the Iroquois camp the first afternoon "not to talk much of the Indians, nor laugh at their dress, nor make any remarks on their behaviour: if we did, it would be very much resented by them, and might cause some differences to arise betwixt the white people and them." Then Commissioner Thomas Lee, alarmed that Maryland, following native protocol, got to speak first because it had first requested the council, tried to bribe Weiser "to influence the Indians to give Virginia the preference before Maryland & to tell them that as they were the oldest Colony, they had a right to have the precedency." Astounded by this breach of their etiquette, the Iroquois refused to go along, replying that they did not care "who was the oldest Colony."[59]

Even when the talks finally got under way, Lee was not done causing "a sort of Confusion." In his opening speech, Canassatego said simply of Virginia that "we have at this present Time nothing to say to him." While Weiser translated these words, "Colo. Lee in an haughty manner interrupted him & said then tell them if they have nothing to say to Us we have nothing to say to them." Lee's outburst brought the proceedings to a screeching halt amid "many disputes." First, the colonists conferred about Lee's "Wrongheadedness" and set him straight. Then Weiser, learning of the southerners' suspicions about him, announced that he would no longer sit in on the Six Nations' private meetings to ponder colonial speeches and prepare a reply. "This created Uneasiness in the Minds of the Indians" and prompted still another secret consultation, during which "Canassatego complain'd they were ill used by the Virginia Strangers" and went on to talk about the possibility of waging war against that province. At last the Indians agreed to return to the treaty ground, in part because Weiser promised "to come to their Councils & to advise with them as in former Treaties." Nonetheless, "confusion" and "deep surprise" still haunted the proceedings. On June 28, Indians were unhappy with the merchandise Maryland offered as payment for the lands in question. The next day's talks stalled as Weiser had to explain the terms of the deal; the day after that, some headmen still refused to sign the document, a "storm," one alarmed colonist wrote, "that threatened to blast our measures."[60]

TREATY MINUTES AS HISTORICAL TEXTS

Almost none of this—not the wrongheadedness or confusion, not the brawlings or wranglings, not the doubts or delays—found its way into the document published by Benjamin Franklin later that summer and reprinted in Part Two. Rather, this sketch of the tortuous road to Lancaster and the squabbles plaguing the council there comes largely from private letters or unpublished journals. That the official record is silent on the shadier, messier aspects of the Lancaster Treaty should prompt readers to wonder more generally about what the account of the formal public proceedings left out, as well as the accuracy of what it included. Of course, any historical document must be approached with caution—all have their biases and blind spots—but caution is even more important when considering an Indian treaty. How well do these pages capture and then convey authentic native voices across the frontier to colonists and across the centuries to us?

There are several issues to keep in mind while reading Franklin's work. One is translation. Conrad Weiser's first language was German, his second was Mohawk, and his third was English. The Iroquois orator Canassatego spoke Onondaga, and his colleague, Gachradodon, spoke Cayuga—Iroquois tongues that were different from (although related to) Weiser's Mohawk. How much got lost when Weiser dragged speeches by an Onondaga and a Cayuga through Mohawk and German to English?

A second issue is the matter of getting Weiser's words down on paper. Imagine if your notes on a lecture were the official record of a class or other talk. How accurate would they be? Now imagine that, while the person speaks, you had to stop writing every so often to sharpen a quill pen's point or dip it into an inkwell. How much would you miss? Quite apart from these obstacles to accurate transcripts, a scribe might deliberately alter or distort Iroquois speeches, either for diplomatic reasons (he did not like what an Indian was saying) or for literary ones (he wanted to sell more copies of the book). At later councils, Reverend Richard Peters mentioned that he went back and revised the rough notes he took during a treaty session to prepare them for publication. How much did he change them in the process?

While consciously shaping the record to suit his own agenda or his own taste, a clerk like Peters unconsciously left out another important feature of councils: The role of Iroquois women in frontier diplomacy. Colonists—who assumed that, in Indian country as in the colonial world, men alone did public business—carefully jotted down the names of all the native men attending the Lancaster Treaty, but they did not list a single woman among the one hundred or so who were there. Some observant Europeans knew that "the women have a deliberative voice in their councils"—indeed that women were "the soul of the councils."[61] It just did not look that way to most colonists, for while native men took the public stage to speak with provincial officials, native women stayed behind the scenes, meeting in private to approve or disapprove proposals and agreements. That they crafted the wampum belts held by orators like Canassatego was tangible, if subtle, proof of their contribution to Iroquois foreign policy. In reading the documents in Part Three, be alert for other signs that women had a larger role in diplomacy than men like Peters knew.

Finally, even the ablest scribe listening to the most gifted interpreter could never get on paper the full richness of these colorful dramas performed by Canassatego, Weiser, and the rest. Studying Franklin's publication is like reading a play instead of watching it, scanning sheet music rather than listening to a recording, or listening to a recording instead of attending a concert. As you make your way through the treaty council proceedings in Part Two, think about what features of those sessions no printed record can transport from the Lancaster courthouse in the sultry summer of 1744 to the present.

Small wonder that students of these documents—historians and linguists, anthropologists and literary critics—have vigorously debated their fidelity to the actual words and events. Some argue that these pages are more Franklin and Peters than Canassatego and Gachradodon. Others are not so sure. "It is amazing, nevertheless, how good the colonial records [of native orations] are," remarked the anthropologist William N. Fenton, who studied Iroquois ways from the 1930s until his death in 2005. Daniel K. Richter, another leading student of the Six Nations, has agreed that "the most valuable clues to Iroquois perspectives come from the speeches native leaders made during diplomatic encounters with Euro-Americans." Because "much of what the Indian speakers intended found its way to paper . . . ," Richter concluded, "they [treaty minutes] are crucial troves of evidence."[62] Once you have read Parts Two and Three, you will be prepared to join this ongoing debate about the quality and accuracy of these fascinating, important historical documents.

THE AFTERMATH OF THE LANCASTER TREATY

As Lancaster's textual treasure trove reveals, for all of the anxiety and tension, the trouble and turmoil that plagued the proceedings, the council ended happily. Conrad Weiser relied on what a provincial leader called "dexterous management" to get all parties to settle land claims and make alliances. Standing between a table of colonists and another of Indians at a banquet, signing on land deeds both *Conrad Weiser* and his newly bestowed Iroquois name, *Tarachiawagon* ("Holder of the Heavens," one of their gods—an indication of the esteem he enjoyed in Iroquoia), Weiser was truly master of ceremonies.[63] As the council drew to a close, "Yo-ha!" and "Huzza!" echoed through the courthouse as the two sides toasted one another, teased Weiser about his beard, and joked about the French. Governor Thomas, Colonel Lee, and the rest even stayed for Canassatego's speech (on July 4, no less!) about their failure to imitate the Iroquois nations and fashion a "Union and a good Agreement" among the squabbling provinces.[64] These officials ignored his advice—days after returning home, they were calling each other names again—but they left Lancaster deeply impressed by Canassatego and his people.[65] "The Indians really appear superior to the [Maryland and Virginia] Commissioners in point of sense and argument," Reverend Peters concluded. But he encouraged readers to study the treaty minutes themselves, which would "raise people's opinions of the wisdom of the Six Nations." These Iroquois, Virginians admitted, possess "strong Traces of good Sense . . . , a noble Simplicity, and . . . manly Fortitude."[66]

Nonetheless, all of the high praise and happy talk hid sinister consequences that made this particular treaty of profound significance, even a turning point, in American history. Buried in the details of the land agreements—details that Weiser might or might not have explained fully to his Iroquois friends—was a bombshell. While Canassatego and his comrades, colonists claimed, "went away well pleased," heading north laden with fine presents and fine words, the documents that their colonial counterparts toted away from Lancaster soon would become weapons of conquest.[67] It turned out that the Iroquois, thinking they had only surrendered claims to the Shenandoah Valley on Virginia's western border, unwittingly gave away (colonists would insist) much of America. Virginians wrote the agreement in such a way that it had natives acknowledging "the right and title of . . . the King of Great Britain to all the lands within the said colony [Virginia] as it is now *or hereafter* may be peopled and bounded by his said Majesty, . . . his heirs and successors." Because the limits of Virginia's original royal charter stretched "from 'sea to sea, west and northwest,'" the Lancaster agreement—in theory, at least—made the Ohio Valley, and every acre stretching from there to the Pacific, part of Virginia![68]

The result was a chain of events that eventually undermined native control of the continent. Within months, officials in Williamsburg started granting huge tracts of western real estate to colonial speculators and settlers, which prompted France to send troops into the Ohio Country to protect its imperial interests and ambitions. This, in turn, brought on the so-called French and Indian War (1754–1763). Beyond that conflict, ultimately, lay the expulsion of many peoples from the heart of North America in a series of brutal wars as native nations, trying to undo what Lancaster had wrought, struggled to maintain their independence and defend their homelands.[69]

Long before then, however, the fragile harmony conjured in Lancaster that summer of 1744 had given way to strife and struggle on the frontier. As treaties and land cessions failed to stop the booming colonial population from encroaching on Indian country—between 1740 and 1760 the number of people in New York and Pennsylvania alone increased from 150,000 to 300,000—natives' disillusionment with their neighbors deepened. Colonists had reasons of their own to be disappointed, for despite earnest proclamations of loyalty to England, most Iroquois sat out the four-year King George's War against France that had started on the eve of the Lancaster congress.[70]

Even "old friends" Canassatego and Conrad Weiser had a falling out. The next time the Onondaga headman led a large delegation to the Pennsylvania frontier en route to talks with provincial officials, during the summer of 1749, a fed-up Weiser refused at first to shake hands with him. "I declare . . . ," the Pennsylvanian complained, "I am altogether tired of Indians, my patience with their behaviour is wore out. I think they grow more insolent now then [*sic*] they have be[e]n before the last Warr, the French and English Courting them So much, made them haughty." Canassatego, snubbed, was no happier. Why, he wondered aloud, have we not received the usual warm welcome from our Pennsylvania friends? "Perhaps it is because you got all our lands that you wanted from us," he told Weiser sternly, "and you dont like to See us any more. . . . We therefore will return to our own Country and give over going to philadelphia, and We Will not trouble our Brethren in philad[elph]ia nor you again."[71]

The two managed to patch things up, but their friendship was near its end. When Weiser arrived in Onondaga for talks the following summer, he learned that Canassatego had just died, probably the victim of an assassination by political foes. (His successor, a Roman Catholic, favored the French.) The wampum belts that signified Iroquois allegiance to England's King George II and his subjects—some of the belts brought home from Lancaster in 1744—were buried with the Onondaga. Did the English flag he flew in front of his house go into the grave as well?[72] Perhaps explaining the tilt toward New France, other Iroquois that very year bluntly expressed their anger at treaties and territory, claiming that the English "used many arts and much cunning, to talk the Indians and their chiefs out of their lands." Before long Indians began accusing Weiser himself of being among those cunning folks whose machinations at Lancaster had cost natives dearly.[73]

During the generation after Canassatego's death, the people of the Six Nations would be able to calculate that cost more precisely. In a way, Lancaster, which at the time looked like just one more in a long series of treaty councils, was in fact a high point of Iroquois power and prestige. After 1750 fewer observers would insist that the Iroquois were "the . . . most formidable People in *North America*." Once the American colonies' war for independence erupted in 1775, contending pressure from Congress and the King would shatter the Six Nations Confederacy. Some Iroquois sided with the rebels, others with the Crown, while still others sought to stay out of the fray altogether. In 1777 the council fire at Onondaga, which had burned so brightly since the very founding of the League, went out.[74]

Seven years later, the victorious Americans broke the Covenant Chain, their long-standing alliance with the Iroquois. At a 1784 treaty, U.S. commissioners began to abandon the rhetoric and rituals that, at Lancaster and every other council for generations, had structured diplomacy between natives and newcomers. "Instead of conforming to the ceremonies practiced in Negociations among the Indians," advised one American leader on the eve of the talks, "it woud be wise to bring them to adopt, gradually, our Forms [and simply tell them]" "it was not the usage of Congress to deliver strings or Belts." He instructed that the U.S. delegation never utter words like "nations" or "Six Nations," for this sort of talk might "revive or seem to confirm their former Ideas of Independence." Even the "Term 'Treaty' . . . seems to[o] much to employ [imply] Equality. . . . They shoud rather be taught . . . that the publick opinion of their importance had long since ceased."

Once talks commenced, American officials interrupted Iroquois orators (a bitter insult) and told them to stop. Then the commissioners delivered their own speeches—most of them by Arthur Lee, son of Colonel Thomas Lee, that "haughty overbearing" fellow who had headed the Virginia delegation at Lancaster four decades before—"in a language by no means accommodating or flattering; quite unlike what they [Iroquois] used to receive." To make matters worse, as the Americans spoke, they "pointed their fingers at the Indians [another insult] to emphasize each instruction."[75]

"It made the Indians stare," wrote one observer. Momentarily stunned, they found their voices soon enough. Far from a conquered or subject people, "we are free, and independent," replied the Iroquois spokesman Kanonraron (Aaron Hill). The Americans were astonished that the Iroquois failed to accept who was now in charge of things. "He indeed assumed all importance in his speech of a[n] emperor . . . ," objected an American who was there. "His assurance was as much as could be borne with, abounding with ridiculous ostentation and arrogance."[76] Divided and dispossessed, Iroquois evidently still considered "themselves *Ongwehoenwe* i.e. Men Surpassing all other men"!

Sustained by that pride and confidence, in the years to come the Iroquois would regain their footing, rekindle their council fire, and restore some semblance of their former unity to forge a future that would not lose touch with their past. Today tens of thousands of Iroquois people live on reservations scattered from upstate New York and lower Canada to northeastern Wisconsin and northeastern Oklahoma, with tens of thousands more in cities and suburbs.[77] Though their everyday lives have changed greatly since Canassatego's day, Iroquois of the twenty-first century have kept alive their ties to ancestors and ancient times. Scattered throughout Iroquois Country today are longhouses, community centers where people gather, as they have for centuries, to connect to one another and to the old ways. During those gatherings, orators speaking Iroquois (and perhaps holding a string or belt of beads) rehearse the saga of Deganawidah and Hiawatha, recalling once more the League's founding. The same slow pace that so annoyed impatient colonists endures. The "Yo-ha!" that echoed through the Lancaster courthouse in 1744 can still be heard.[78]

In addition, Iroquois diplomats—Canassatego's successors—still leave the longhouse and the reservation to negotiate with outsiders in courtrooms and legislative chambers from Albany, New York, to Washington, D.C., and beyond. As if to demonstrate the abiding power and continuing relevance of his people's diplomatic culture and customs, in 1988 an Iroquois ambassador stood before the United Nations Human Rights Commission at Geneva, Switzerland, wampum belt in hand, to explain how the Six Nations—the first "United Nations"— had conducted talks between groups.[79] The envoy was recalling a time when peoples from different worlds came together to resolve their differences with beaded strings in hand rather than a musket or tomahawk. If the Lancaster Treaty of 1744 was contentious (and it was), if its seemingly happy ending hid fundamental differences that would reappear soon enough (and it did), it nonetheless stands as a moment when foreigners sought peaceful resolution of their differences. In our own day, when understanding across frontiers of language, faith, and culture is too rare and moments of accord between peoples too few, it is worth revisiting Lancaster and listening once again to the people gathered there.

NOTES

[1] Document 4, pp. 110–11 (description of Canassatego), p. 122 ("famous orator"). Julian P. Boyd, "Indian Affairs in Pennsylvania, 1736–1762," in Boyd, ed., *Indian Treaties Printed by Benjamin Franklin, 1736–1762* (Philadelphia: Historical Society of Pennsylvania, 1938), xl ("much admired"). The courthouse could hold "above 800 persons" (Document 4, p. 109). For Iroquois speakers walking to and fro and singing their speeches, see Document 2, p. 94, and Document 3, p. 101. The best biography of this Iroquois leader is William A. Starna, "The Diplomatic Career of Canasatego," in William A. Pencak and Daniel K. Richter, eds., *Friends and Enemies in Penn's Woods: Indians, Colonists, and the Racial Construction of Pennsylvania* (University Park: Pennsylvania State University Press, 2004), ch. 8. The spelling of his name varies widely; I use the version employed in the principal text (see Part Two).

[2] See Treaty, pp. 53–54. It was Iroquois custom to address the leader of a colony even if that leader was not actually there in person. They expected his representative to take the words back to the governor.

[3] Lawrence Wroth, "The Indian Treaty as Literature," *Yale Review*, 17 (1928): 762; Carl Van Doren, "Introduction," in Boyd, ed., *Indian Treaties*, viii.

[4] Document 4, p. 126.

[5] William N. Fenton, *The Great Law and the Longhouse: A Political History of the Iroquois Confederacy* (Norman: University of Oklahoma Press, 1998), 423 ("virtuoso performance"); Boyd, "Indian Affairs," in Boyd, ed., *Indian Treaties*, xl (Peters); Leonard W. Labaree, ed., *The Papers of Benjamin Franklin*, II (New Haven, Conn.: Yale University Press, 1960), 411 (Franklin); Witham Marshe, "Journal of the Treaty Held with the Six Nations . . . at Lancaster, in Pennsylvania, June, 1744," *Collections of the Massachusetts Historical Society, for the Year M,DCCC* (Boston, 1801), 1st Series, Volume 7, 177, 201 (Lancaster). For the treaty's publishing history, see J. A. Leo Lemay, *The Life of Benjamin Franklin*, Volume Two, *Printer and Publisher, 1730–1747* (Philadelphia: University of Pennsylvania Press, 2006), 394–95; Sandra M. Gustafson, *Eloquence Is Power: Oratory and Performance in Early America* (Chapel Hill: University of North Carolina Press, 2000), 119.

[6] Fenton, *Great Law*, 423. See also Paul A. W. Wallace, *Conrad Weiser, 1696–1760: Friend of Colonist and Mohawk* (Philadelphia: University of Pennsylvania Press, 1945), 185.

[7] An excellent account of this treaty is Timothy J. Shannon, *Indians and Colonists at the Crossroads of Empire: The Albany Congress of 1754* (Ithaca, N.Y.: Cornell University Press, 2000).

[8] Two good general treatments of this field are Colin Calloway, *New Worlds for All: Indians, Europeans, and the Remaking of Early America* (Baltimore: Johns Hopkins University Press, 1997), and Daniel K. Richter, *Facing East from Indian Country: A Native History of Early America* (Cambridge, Mass.: Harvard University Press, 2001).

[9] Quoted in James H. Merrell, *Into the American Woods: Negotiators on the Pennsylvania Frontier* (New York: W. W. Norton, 1999), 19.

[10]See James H. Merrell, "'The Customes of Our Countrey': Indians and Colonists in Early America," in Bernard Bailyn and Philip D. Morgan, eds., *Strangers within the Realm: Cultural Margins of the First British Empire* (Chapel Hill: University of North Carolina Press, 1991), 117–56. For "Indian Attornies," see Merrell, *American Woods*, 104.

[11]Carl Bridenbaugh, ed., *Gentleman's Progress: The* Itinerarium *of Dr. Alexander Hamilton, 1744* (Pittsburgh: University of Pittsburgh Press, 1948), 34, 98, 110, 112–14, 172. The ten nations were five of the six Iroquois nations (no Mohawks attended—their leaders were in Boston at the time), along with allied groups, the Conestogas, Conoys, Nanticokes, Saponis, and Shawnees. See *Pennsylvania Archives*, 1st Series, Volume I (Harrisburg, Pa.: Joseph Severns and Company, 1852), 656–57 (hereafter cited as *Penn. Arch.*).

[12]Document 4, pp. 110, 122.

[13]Merrell, *American Woods*, 253–54; Richard White, *The Middle Ground: Indians, Empires, and Republics in the Great Lakes Region, 1650–1815* (New York: Cambridge University Press, 1991).

[14]Richter, "Ordeals of the Longhouse: The Five Nations in Early American History," in Daniel K. Richter and James H. Merrell, eds., *Beyond the Covenant Chain: The Iroquois and Their Neighbors in Indian North America, 1600–1800* (University Park: Pennsylvania State University Press, 2004), 16. See also Richter, *The Ordeal of the Longhouse: The Peoples of the Iroquois League in the Era of European Colonization* (Chapel Hill: University of North Carolina Press, 1992), ch. 2; Fenton, *Great Law*, Parts 1 and 2; Dean R. Snow, *The Iroquois*, The Peoples of America Series (Cambridge, Mass.: Blackwell, 1994), ch. 4.

[15]Quoted in Richter, *Ordeal of the Longhouse*, 31.

[16]Quoted in ibid., 39, 47.

[17]For one theory on the origins and meaning of the word *Iroquois*, see Snow, *The Iroquois*, 1–2.

[18]Quoted in Richter, *Ordeal of the Longhouse*, 43.

[19]Document 3, p. 100.

[20]Mary A. Druke, "Linking Arms: The Structure of Iroquois Tribal Diplomacy," in Richter and Merrell, eds., *Beyond the Covenant Chain*, ch. 2.

[21]Richter, "Ordeals of the Longhouse," in ibid., ch. 1; Richter, *Ordeal of the Longhouse* ("spiritual unity," 170); Fenton, *Great Law*, 425 (no League Sachems at Lancaster).

[22]Mathew Dennis, *Cultivating a Landscape of Peace: Iroquois-European Encounters in Seventeenth-Century America* (Ithaca, N.Y.: Cornell University Press, 1993).

[23]Quoted in Fenton, *Great Law*, 409.

[24]Francis Jennings, *The Ambiguous Iroquois Empire: The Covenant Chain Confederation of Indian Tribes with English Colonies from Its Beginnings to the Lancaster Treaty of 1744* (New York: W. W. Norton, 1984); Richter, *Ordeal of the Longhouse*.

[25]See Richard Aquila, *The Iroquois Restoration: Iroquois Diplomacy on the Colonial Frontier, 1701–1754* (Detroit: Wayne State University Press, 1983), ch. 6; Jennings, *Ambiguous Iroquois Empire*; Richter, *Ordeal of the Longhouse*, chs. 9–10; Fenton, *Great Law*, ch. 26. A good summary of Iroquois treaties is "Descriptive Treaty Calendar," in Francis Jennings, ed., *The History and Culture of Iroquois Diplomacy: An Interdisciplinary Guide to the Treaties of the Six Nations and Their League* (Syracuse, N.Y.: Syracuse University Press, 1985), ch. 8.

[26]Treaty, p. 86. Richter, *Ordeal of the Longhouse*, ch. 11; Fenton, *Great Law*, 408–9; Starna, "Canasatego," in Pencak and Richter, eds., *Friends and Enemies*, 145–47.

[27]Treaty, pp. 46–47 (Thomas); quoted in Fenton, *Great Law*, 409 ("gone").

[28]Alden Vaughan, gen. ed., *Early American Indian Documents: Treaties and Laws, 1607–1789*, Volume IX, *New York and New Jersey Treaties, 1714–1753*, ed. Barbara Graymont (Bethesda, Md.: University Publications of America, 1996), 323.

[29]Jennings, *Ambiguous Iroquois Empire*, 356; Fenton, *Great Law*, 422–24. The Six Nations did originally propose Conodoguinet, an abandoned Indian town across the

Susquehanna River, but they acceded to the colonists' suggestion that nearby Lancaster would be better able to feed and house the hundreds of people expected.

[30] *Minutes of the Provincial Council of Pennsylvania, From the Organization to the Termination of the Proprietary Government*, Volume IV (Harrisburg, Pa.: Theo. Fenn & Co., 1851), 563 (hereafter cited as *MPCP*).

[31] Richter, *Ordeal of the Longhouse*, 40–42; Merrell, *American Woods*, 31–32, 254–55.

[32] Quoted in Merrell, *American Woods*, 265; Document 2, p. 95. Bartram specifically mentioned the 1744 Lancaster treaty as an example of the delay in replying.

[33] *MPCP*, IV, 80.

[34] *Treaty*, p. 47.

[35] Quoted in Merrell, *American Woods*, 188–89; and see Richter, *Facing East*, 137.

[36] Gooch to [Thomas Lee], June 14, 1744, in Paul P. Hoffman, ed., *The Lee Family Papers, 1742–1795* (microfilm, Charlottesville: University of Virginia Library, 1966), Reel 1; *Penn. Arch.*, 1st Ser., I, 649. Also see Document 3.

[37] Shoemaker, *A Strange Likeness: Becoming Red and White in Eighteenth-Century North America* (New York: Oxford University Press, 2004), 3.

[38] Merrell, *American Woods*, 274–75.

[39] Gustafson, *Eloquence Is Power*, 121.

[40] *MPCP*, IV, 88.

[41] Ibid., 581, 661.

[42] Thomas to Gooch (copy), Jan. 20, 1743/4, Richard Peters Papers, II, Part 1, p. 2, Historical Society of Pennsylvania, Philadelphia (hereafter cited as HSP). Edmund Jenings to the Board of Trade, June 12, 1744, Calvert Papers, Mss. 174, No. 1109, Maryland Historical Society, Baltimore (copy in Francis Jennings et al., eds., *Iroquois Indians: A Documentary History of the Six Nations and Their League* [microfilm, Woodbridge, Conn.: Research Publications, 1984], reel 12, June 12, 1744); *MPCP*, IV, 649.

[43] Merrell, *American Woods*, 137, 141–42.

[44] Quoted in ibid., 292 ("Running," "Fraud"); Delaware Indians "To Mr Jeremiah Langhorne & all Magistrates in Pennsylvania," Nov. 21, 1740, and Delaware Indians to Gov. Thomas, Jan. 3, 1741, in Penn Manuscripts, Indian Affairs, Vol. IV, p. 30, HSP. See Steven Craig Harper, *Promised Land: Penn's Holy Experiment, the Walking Purchase, and the Dispossession of Delawares, 1600–1763* (Bethlehem, Pa.: Lehigh University Press, 2006).

[45] *MPCP*, IV, 570, 579–80.

[46] Aquila, *Iroquois Restoration*, 180–82; Jennings, *Ambiguous Iroquois Empire*, 322–24, 356–62; Starna, "Canasatego," in Pencak and Richter, eds., *Friends and Enemies*, 154 ("bogus"). For a view that gives more credit to Iroquois claims, see Susan Kalter, "Introduction," in Kalter, ed., *Benjamin Franklin, Pennsylvania, and the First Nations: The Treaties of 1736–62* (Urbana: University of Illinois Press, 2006), 21–23. The Iroquois request is in Vaughan, gen. ed., *Early Am. Indian Docs.*, I, *Pennsylvania and Delaware Treaties, 1629–1737*, ed. Donald H. Kent (Washington, D.C.: University Publications of America, 1979), 445–46.

[47] *MPCP*, IV, 94, 570–71.

[48] *Archives of Maryland* [Online], XXVIII, 257–71 (quotation on 260); Marshe, "Journal," 199–200; C. A. Weslager, *The Nanticoke Indians—Past and Present* (Newark: University of Delaware Press, 1983), ch. 9.

[49] Merrell, *American Woods*, 168–71; *MPCP*, IV, 635.

[50] Merrell, *American Woods*, 171–75; *MPCP*, IV, 634, 665 ("Dark Cloud"). For two accounts of Weiser's work, see Documents 2 and 3. "Bury the hatchet" is Peters, quoted in Boyd, "Indian Affairs," in Boyd, ed., *Indian Treaties*, xxxv.

[51] Merrell, *American Woods*, 42–53; *Penn. Arch.*, 1st ser., I, 647 ("quarrel with you").

[52] This conflict, which lasted four years, was called "King George's War" in the colonies and the "War of the Austrian Succession" in Europe.

[53]*MPCP*, IV, 564; Boyd, "Indian Affairs," in Boyd, ed., *Indian Treaties*, xxxvii ("interesting").

[54]Boyd, "Indian Affairs," in Boyd, ed., *Indian Treaties*, xxxvi ("no thoughts"); R. Alonzo Brock, ed., "Journal of William Black, 1744 . . . ," *Pennsylvania Magazine of History and Biography*, I (1877): 129 ("infected"); Peters to Thomas Penn, Aug. 2, 1744, Richard Peters Letterbook, 1737–1750, 249–50, Richard Peters Papers, HSP.

[55]Quoted in Wallace, *Weiser*, 197 ("overbearing"); Peters to Penn, Aug. 2, 1744, Peters Letterbook, 1737–1750, 250 ("vent"); quoted in Boyd, "Indian Affairs," in Boyd, ed., *Indian Treaties*, xxxvii ("flaming," "doubt").

[56]Document 3, p. 106; Fenton, *Great Law*, 424.

[57]Thomas to Gooch, Jan. 20, 1743/44 (copy), Peters Papers, II, Part 1, p. 2; Peters to Weiser, June 11, 1744, ibid., 14 ("anxiety," "impatient"); Brock, ed., "Journal of Black," *Pa. Mag. Hist. and Biography*, I (1877): 129 (doubt).

[58]Marshe, "Journal," 172 ("rum"; "eggs and bacon"), 173 (barbers), 178 (bugs, water); *Penn. Arch.*, 1st ser., I, 658 (backgammon tables).

[59]Document 4, p. 111; ("not to talk"); Peters to Penn, Aug. 2, 1744, Peters Letterbook, 1737–1750, 253.

[60]Peters to Penn, Aug. 2, 1744, Peters Letterbook, 1737–1750, 252–53; Document 4, p. 124.

[61]Fenton, *Great Law*, 215; Barbara Alice Mann, *Iroquoian Women: The Gantowisas* (New York: P. Lang, 2000), 120.

[62]Fenton, *Great Law*, 8; Richter, *Ordeal of the Longhouse*, 5–6. And see James H. Merrell, "'I desire all that I have said . . . may be taken down aright': Revisiting Teedyuscung's 1756 Treaty Council Speeches," *William and Mary Quarterly*, 3rd Series, 63 (2006): 777–826.

[63]Document 4, p. 124.

[64]Treaty, p. 85. Recently some scholars, quoting such advice, have argued that the Iroquois served as a model for Benjamin Franklin and other Founding Fathers who later drafted the United States Constitution. The argument over the "Iroquois influence thesis" has generated considerable controversy, but the evidence for a direct, powerful effect is slight. See Bruce E. Johansen, *Forgotten Founders: How the American Indian Helped Shape Democracy* (Harvard and Boston, Mass.: The Harvard Common Press, 1982); Elisabeth Tooker, "The United States Constitution and the Iroquois League," *Ethnohistory*, 35 (1988): 305–36; Donald A. Grinde Jr. and Bruce E. Johansen, *Exemplar of Liberty: Native America and the Evolution of Democracy* (Los Angeles: American Indian Studies Center, University of California–Los Angeles, 1991); William A. Starna and George R. Hamell, "History and the Burden of Proof: The Case of Iroquois Influence on the U.S. Constitution," *New York History*, 77 (1996): 427–52; "Forum: The 'Iroquois Influence' Thesis—Con and Pro," *William and Mary Quarterly*, 3rd Series, 53 (1996): 587–636; Kalter, "Introduction," in Kalter, ed., *Franklin, Pennsylvania, and the First Nations*, 23–29.

[65]Peters to Penn, Aug. 2, 1744, Peters Letterbook, 1737–1750, 249–53; Document 4, p. 126. Vaughan, gen. ed., *Early Am. Indian Docs.*, Volume VI, *Maryland Treaties, 1632–1775*, ed. W. Stitt Robinson (Frederick, Md.: University Publications of America, 1987), 267–68.

[66]Boyd, "Indian Affairs," in Boyd, ed., *Indian Treaties*, xl (Peters); quoted in Fenton, *Great Law*, 437.

[67]Richard Hockley to Thomas Penn, Aug. 2, 1744, Penn Manuscripts, Official Correspondence, v. 4, p. 13, HSP.

[68]Jennings, *Ambiguous Iroquois Empire*, 361.

[69]Ibid., 360–66; Jennings, "Iroquois Alliances in American History," in Jennings, ed., *Iroquois Diplomacy*, 46–48; Jennings, *Empire of Fortune: Crowns, Colonies, and Tribes in the Seven Years War in America* (New York: W. W. Norton, 1988); Gregory Evans Dowd,

A Spirited Resistance: The North American Indian Struggle for Unity, 1745–1815 (Baltimore: Johns Hopkins University Press, 1992).

[70]Jennings, *Empire of Fortune*, ch. 2; Aquila, *Iroquois Restoration*, 92–101.

[71]"Old friends" is Weiser's term for Canassatego and others he saw at Albany in 1745. See Starna, "Canasatego," in Pencak and Richter, eds., *Friends and Enemies*, 156. Weiser to Peters, Aug. 6, 1749, Eugene Du Simitiere Papers, 966.F.26a, Library Company of Philadelphia ("tired"); "Memorandum at Council held the 7 of August Canassatego Speaker about 36 Indians," Peters Papers, II, 122; Wallace, *Weiser*, ch. 34; Fenton, *Great Law*, 436–37; Gustafson, *Eloquence Is Power*, 137.

[72]Wallace, *Weiser*, ch. 38; Jennings, *Ambiguous Iroquois Empire*, 363–65; Fenton, *Great Law*, 459; William M. Beauchamp, ed., *Moravian Journals Relating to Central New York, 1745–66* (Syracuse, N.Y.: The Dehler Press, 1916), 46, 93 ("flag").

[73]Beauchamp, ed., *Moravian Journals*, 25, 45 ("arts"). In 1752 an Iroquois spokesman at a treaty in the Ohio Country told Virginians that "we never understood, before you told us Yesterday, that the Lands then sold [at Lancaster in 1744] were to extend further to the Sun setting than the Hill on the other Side of the Allegany Hill." See "The Treaty of Logg's Town, 1752," *Virginia Magazine of History and Biography*, XIII (1905–1906): 160–61, 167–68, 173–74 (quotation on 168).

[74]Barbara Graymont, *The Iroquois in the American Revolution* (Syracuse, N.Y.: Syracuse University Press, 1972), chs. 5–6.

[75]Vaughan, gen. ed., *Early Am. Ind. Treaties and Documents*, XVIII, *Revolution and Confederation*, ed. Colin G. Calloway (Bethesda, Md.: University Publications of America, 1994), 299–301, and 590 n.33; Anthony F. C. Wallace, *The Death and Rebirth of the Seneca* (New York: Vintage Books, 1972), 197–98. For discussions of this treaty, see Fenton, *Great Law*, Parts 5–6; Graymont, *Iroquois in the American Revolution*, ch. 10.

[76]Wallace, *Death and Rebirth*, 198 ("stare"); Graymont, *Iroquois in the American Revolution*, 280–81 (Hill).

[77]Surveys of Iroquois Country in recent times can be found in Snow, *The Iroquois*, ch. 13, and William Engelbrecht, *Iroquoia: The Development of a Native World* (Syracuse, N.Y.: Syracuse University Press, 2003), ch. 9. The 2000 U.S. census counted almost 81,000 Iroquois.

[78]Fenton, *Great Law*, 11–12 ("pace"), 51 ("saga"), 187, 427 ("Yo-ha!").

[79]Robert A. Williams, Jr., *Linking Arms Together: American Indian Treaty Visions of Law and Peace, 1600–1800* (New York: Routledge, 1999), 4.

PART TWO

The Document

A NOTE ABOUT THE TEXT

Benjamin Franklin published the following text of the Lancaster Treaty in the late summer of 1744. (The September 6 issue of his newspaper, the *Pennsylvania Gazette*, advertised it for sale.) This large edition (or "folio"), with pages about 10 inches wide and 15 inches tall, was reproduced, in facsimile, by Julian P. Boyd in a volume entitled *Indian Treaties Printed by Benjamin Franklin, 1736–1762* (Philadelphia: Historical Society of Pennsylvania, 1938), pp. 41–79. What follows here is drawn from Boyd's reproduction of the original, checked against the 1744 edition in Early American Imprints, Series I: Evans, no. 5416, Readex Digital Collections, another photographic reproduction of the 1744 original. I have left intact all of Franklin's editorial decisions, including capitalization and italics that differ from current practices, changing here and in Documents 2 and 4 only the "long s" that was common at that time (which looked something like ∫—thus making *Canassatego* into *Cana∫∫atego* and *Weiser* into *Wei∫er*).

A
TREATY,

Held at the Town of
Lancaster, in Pennsylvania,
By the Honourable the
Lieutenant-Governor of the PROVINCE,
And the Honourable the
Commissioners for the PROVINCES
OF
Virginia *and* Maryland,
WITH THE

INDIANS

Of

the

SIX NATIONS,

In *JUNE*, 1744.

PHILADELPHIA:
Printed and Sold by B. FRANKLIN, at the New-Printing-Office,
near the Market. M,DCC,XLIV.*

*(See Figure 5.)

Julian P. Boyd, ed., *Indian Treaties Printed by Benjamin Franklin, 1736–1762* (Philadelphia: Historical Society of Pennsylvania, 1938), 41–79.

A

TREATY,

Held at the Town of

Lancaster, in PENNSYLVANIA,

By the HONOURABLE the

Lieutenant-Governor of the PROVINCE,

And the HONOURABLE the

Commiſſioners for the PROVINCES

OF

VIRGINIA *and* MARYLAND,

WITH THE

INDIANS

OF THE

SIX NATIONS,

In *JUNE*, 1744.

PHILADELPHIA:
Printed and Sold by B. FRANKLIN, at the New-Printing-Office,
near the Market. M,DCC,XLIV.

42

A

TREATY

WITH THE
INDIANS
OF THE
SIX NATIONS.

In the Court-House in the Town of *Lancaster*, on *Friday*, the Twenty Second of *June*, 1744,

PRESENT,

The Honourable *GEORGE THOMAS*, Esq; Lieut. Governor of the Province of *Pennsylvania*, and Counties of *Newcastle, Kent* and *Sussex*, on *Delaware*.[1]

The Honourable *Thomas Lee*, Esq; \
Colonel *William Beverly*,[2] } Commissioners of *Virginia*.

[1] *Delaware*: In 1744 the three counties that later became Delaware were part of Pennsylvania.

[2] *William Beverly* (c. 1673–c. 1760): In 1744 Beverly was a member of the Virginia House of Burgesses, the provincial legislature.

Opposite: **Figure 5**   *A Treaty, Held at the Town of Lancaster, in Pennsylvania* . . .
Title page of Benjamin Franklin's edition of the treaty minutes. The Pennsylvania Assembly paid Franklin to produce about one hundred copies of the Lancaster Treaty for distribution to colonial and imperial officials. Ever the enterprising businessman, Franklin printed 300 more copies for sale in England and another 600 or so to be sold in England's American colonies. The thirty-nine-page volume, called a "folio," was an impressive (and expensive) size, measuring 10″ × 15½″. Before the end of the year, William Parks, a printer in Williamsburg, Virginia, produced a similar but not identical version of the proceedings for sale there. The preface to that edition proved so "instructive and entertaining" (to use Parks's self-serving claims!) that in December 1744 it was reprinted in London's *American Magazine*.

A Treaty, Held at the Town of Lancaster, *in Pennsylvania, By the Honourable the Lieutenant-Governor of the Province, And the Honourable the Commissioners for the Provinces of* Virginia *and* Maryland, *With the* Indians *of the Six Nations, In June, 1744*. Philadelphia: B. Franklin, 1744. Image courtesy of The Library Company of Philadelphia.

The Honble *Edmund Jennings*,[3] Esq;
Philip Thomas,[4] Esq;
Colonel *Robert King*,[5]
Colonel *Thomas Colville*,[6]

} Commissioners of *Maryland*.

The Deputies of the *Onandagoes, Senecas, Cayogoes, Oneidas* and *Tuscaroraes*.
Conrad Weiser, Interpreter.

THE Governor and the Commissioners took some of the *Indian* Chiefs by the Hand, and, after they had seated themselves, the Governor bid them welcome into the Government; and there being Wine and Punch prepared for them, the Governor and the several Commissioners drank Health to the *Six Nations*; and *Canassatego, Tachanoontia*, and some other Chiefs, returned the Compliments, drinking the Healths of **Onas, †Assaragoa*, and the Governor of *Maryland*.

AFTER they were all served with Wine, Punch, Pipes and Tobacco, the Governor told the *Indians*, that as it was customary, and indeed necessary, they should have some Time to rest after so long a Journey, and as he thought three Days would be no more than sufficient for that Purpose, he proposed to speak to them on *Monday* next; after which, the honourable Commissioners would take their own Time to deliver what they had to say.

CANASSATEGO answered the Governor: We thank you for giving us Time to rest; we are come to you, and shall leave it intirely to you to appoint the Time when we shall meet you again. We likewise leave it to the Governor of *Maryland*, by whose Invitation we came here, to appoint a Time when he will please to mention the Reason of his inviting us. As to our Brother *Assaragoa*, we have at this present Time nothing to say to him; not but we have a great deal to say to *Assaragoa*, which must be said at one Time or another; but not being

---

[3] *Edmund Jennings* (?–1756): A leading Maryland official who was then a member of the Provincial Council.

[4] *Philip Thomas* (1694–1762): A prominent planter and member of the Provincial Council.

[5] *Robert King* (1689–1755): A planter and member of the Lower House of Assembly.

[6] *Thomas Colville* (c. 1688–1766): A merchant, and a member of the Lower House of Assembly.

*Onas, the Governor of *Pennsylvania*. [Franklin note.]

†*Assaragoa*, the Governor of *Virginia*. [Franklin note.]

satisfied whether he or we should begin first, we shall leave it wholly to our Brother *Onas* to adjust this between us, and to say which shall begin first.

In the COURT-HOUSE at *Lancaster, June* 25, 1744. *A. M.*

P R E S E N T ,

The Honourable *GEORGE THOMAS,* Esq; Governor, &c.
The Honourable the Commissioners of *Virginia.*
The Honourable the Commissioners of *Maryland.*
The Deputies of the *Six Nations.*
Conrad Weiser, Interpreter.

The GOVERNOR spoke as follows:

Honourable Gentlemen, Commissioners for the Governments of Virginia *and* Maryland, *and Brethren, Sachims, or Chiefs of the* Indians *of the* Six Nations:

A T a Treaty, held by me two Years ago, in Behalf of the Government of *Pennsylvania,* with a Number of the Chiefs of the *Indians* of the *Six Nations,* I was desired by them to write to the Governor of *Maryland* concerning some Lands in the back Parts of that Province, which they claim a Right to from their Conquests over the ancient Possessors, and which have been settled by some of the Inhabitants of that Government, without their Consent, or any Purchase made from them. It was at that time understood that the Claim was upon *Maryland* only; but it has since appeared, by some Letters formerly wrote by Mr. President *Logan*[7] to the late Governor of *Maryland,* that it related likewise to some Lands in the back Parts of *Virginia.* The Governors of those Colonies soon manifested a truly equitable Disposition to come to any reasonable Terms with the *Six Nations* on account of those Lands, and desired, that for that End a Time and Place might be fixed for a Treaty with them; but before this could be effected, an unfortunate Skirmish happened in the back Parts of *Virginia,* between some of the Militia there, and a Party of the *Indian* Warriors of the *Six Nations,* with some Loss on both Sides. Who were the Aggressors is

---

[7] *Logan:* James Logan (1674–1751) the Penn family's agent in the province during the first few decades of the eighteenth century, a member of the Provincial Council, a leading merchant, and an architect of the colony's Indian policy.

not at this time to be discussed, both Parties having agreed to bury that Affair in Oblivion, and the Government of *Virginia* having, in Token of the Continuance of their Friendship, presented the *Six Nations*, through my Hands, with Goods to the Value of One Hundred Pounds Sterling. To prevent further Hostilities, and to heal this Breach, I had, before the Present was given, made a Tender of my good Offices; which both Parties accepted, and consented, on my Instances, to lay down their Arms: Since which the Faith pledged to me has been mutually preserved, and a Time and Place has been agreed upon, through my Intervention, for accommodating all Differences, and for settling a firm Peace, Union and Friendship, as well between the Government of *Virginia* as that of *Maryland*, and the *Indians* of the *Six Nations**. The honourable the Commissioners for these two Governments, and the Deputies of the *Six Nations*, are now met at the Place appointed for the Treaty. It only remains therefore for me to say, That if my further good Offices shall be thought useful for the Accomplishment of this Work, you may rely most assuredly upon them.

BUT I hope, honourable Gentlemen Commissioners, it will not be taken amiss if I go a little further, and briefly represent to you, how especially necessary it is at this Juncture, for his Majesty's Service, and the Good of all his Colonies in this Part of his Dominions, that Peace and Friendship be established between your Governments and the *Indians* of the *Six Nations*.

THESE *Indians*, by their Situation, are a Frontier to some of them; and, from thence, if Friends, are capable of defending their Settlements; if Enemies, of making cruel Ravages upon them; if Neuters [neutrals], they may deny the *French* a Passage through their Country, and give us timely Notice of their Designs. These are but some of the Motives for cultivating a good Understanding with them; but from hence the Disadvantages of a Rupture are abundantly evident. Every Advantage you gain over them in War will be a weakening of the Barrier of those Colonies, and consequently be, in effect, Victories over yourselves and your Fellow Subjects. Some Allowances for their Prejudices and Passions, and a Present now and then for the Relief of their Necessities, which have, in some Measure, been brought upon them by their Intercourse with us, and by our yearly extending our Settlements, will probably tie them more closely to the *British* Interest. This has been the Method of *New-York* and *Pennsylvania*, and will not put

---

*This was allowed, at a Conference had by the Governor with the Commissioners, to be a just State of the Transactions preceding the Treaty. [Franklin note.]

you to so much Expence in twenty Years, as the carrying on a War against them will do in one. The *French* very well know the Importance of these Nations to us, and will not fail by Presents, and their other usual Arts, to take Advantage of any Misunderstandings we may have with them*. But I will detain you, Gentlemen, no longer. Your own superior Knowledge will suggest to you more than I can say on this Subject.

Friends and Brethren, Sachims, or Chiefs of the Indians *of the* Six Nations:

THESE, your Brethren of *Virginia* and *Maryland*, are come to enlarge the Fire, which was almost gone out, and to make it burn clearer; to brighten the Chain which had contracted some Rust, and to renew their Friendship with you; which it is their Desire may last so long as the Sun, the Moon and the Stars, shall give Light. Their Powers are derived from the *Great King of* ENGLAND, your Father; and whatever Conclusions they shall come to with you, will be as firm and binding as if the Governors of these Provinces were themselves here. I am your Brother, and, which is more, I am your true Friend. As you know, from Experience, that I am so, I will now give you a few Words of Advice. Receive these your Brethren with open Arms; unite yourselves to them in the Covenant Chain, and be you with them as one Body, and one Soul. I make no doubt but the Governor of *Canada* has been taking Pains to widen the Breach between these your Brethren of *Virginia* and you; but as you cannot have forgot the Hatred the *French* have always borne to your Nations, and how kindly, on the contrary, you have been treated, and how faithfully you have been protected by the *Great King of* ENGLAND and his Subjects, you will not be at a Loss to see into the Designs of that Governor. He wants to divide you from us, in order the more easily to destroy you, which he will most certainly do, if you suffer yourselves to be deluded by him.

As to what relates to the Friendship established between the Government of *Pennsylvania* and your Nations, I will take another Day to speak to you upon it.

---

*The two preceding Paragraphs were allowed by the Commissioners of *Virginia*, whilst they were at *Philadelphia* [before the treaty], to be very proper to be spoke by the Governor of *Pennsylvania* at the Opening of the Treaty; but taking up an Opinion, from what passed at the first friendly Interview with the *Indians*, that they would not make any Claim upon Lands within the Government of *Virginia*, the Governor consented to decline speaking them in the Presence of the *Indians*. [Franklin note.]

To enforce what had been said, the GOVERNOR *laid down a Belt of Wampum; upon which the* Indians *gave the* *Yo-hah.

AFTER a short Pause, the Governor ordered the Interpreter to tell the *Indians,* that as they had greatly exceeded their appointed Time for meeting the Commissioners, he recommended to them to use all the Expedition possible in giving their Answer to what had been said, that they might forthwith proceed to treat with the respective Commissioners on the Business they came about.

THEN *Canassatego* repeated to the Interpreter the Substance of what the Governor had spoke, in order to know if he had understood him right (a Method generally made use of by the *Indians*) and when the Interpreter told him he had taken the true Sense, *Canassatego* proceeded to return the Thanks of the *Six Nations* for the Governor's kind Advice, promising to follow it as far as lay in their Power; but as it was their Custom when a Belt was given to return another, they would take Time till the Afternoon to provide one, and would then give their Answer.

In the COURT-HOUSE at *Lancaster, June* 25, 1744. *P. M.*

P R E S E N T,

The Honourable *GEORGE THOMAS*, Esq; Governor, &c.
The Honourable the Commissioners of *Virginia.*
The Honourable the Commissioners of *Maryland.*
The Deputies of the *Six Nations.*
Conrad Weiser, Interpreter.

Canassatego's *Answer to the Governor's Speech delivered in the Morning.*

Brother Onas,

YOU spoke in the Presence of *Assaragoa* and the Governor of *Maryland* to us, advising us to receive them as our Brethren, and to unite with them in the Covenant Chain as one Body, and one Soul. We have always considered them as our Brethren, and, as such, shall be willing to brighten the Chain of Friendship with them; but since there are some Disputes between us respecting the Lands possessed by them, which formerly belonged to us, we, according to our Custom,

---

*The *Yo-hah* denotes Approbation, being a loud Shout or Cry, consisting of a few Notes pronounced by all the *Indians* in a very musical Manner, in the Nature of our Huzza's. [Franklin note.]

propose to have those Differences first adjusted, and then we shall proceed to confirm the Friendship subsisting between us, which will meet with no Obstruction after these Matters are settled.

Here they presented the GOVERNOR *with a Belt of Wampum, in return for the Belt given them in the Morning by the* GOVERNOR; *and the Interpreter was ordered to return the* Yo-hah.

Then the GOVERNOR, *in Reply, spoke as follows:*

I receive your Belt with great Kindness and Affection; and as to what relates to the Governments of *Virginia* and *Maryland*, the honourable Commissioners, now present, are ready to treat with you. I shall only add, that the Goods for the Hundred Pounds Sterling, put into my Hands by the Governor of *Virginia*, as a Token of his good Dispositions to preserve Friendship with you, are now in Town, and ready to be delivered, in consequence of what was told you by *Conrad Weiser* when he was last at *Onandago*.

THEN the Governor, turning to the Commissioners of *Virginia* and *Maryland*, said, Gentlemen, I have now finished what was incumbent upon me to say by way of Introduction to the *Indians*; and as you have a full Authority from your respective Governments to treat with them, I shall leave the rest intirely to you, and either stay or withdraw, as you shall think most for your Service.

THE Commissioners said, They were all of Opinion, it would be for their Advantage that the Governor should stay with them; and therefore they unanimously desired he would favour them with the Continuance of his Presence whilst they should be in Treaty with the *Indians*: Which his Honour said he would at their Instance very readily do, believing it might expedite their Business, and prevent any Jealousy the *Indians* might conceive at his withdrawing.

The Commissioners of Maryland *ordered the Interpreter to acquaint the* Indians *that the Governor of* Maryland *was going to speak to them, and then spoke as follows:*

Friends and Brethren of the united Six Nations,

WE, who are deputed from the Government of *Maryland* by a Commission under the Great Seal of that Province, now in our Hands (and which will be interpreted to you) bid you welcome; and in Token that we are very glad to see you here as Brethren, we give you this String of Wampum.

Upon which the Indians gave the Yo-hah.

WHEN the Governor of *Maryland* received the first Notice, about seven Years ago, of your Claim to some Lands in that Province, he thought our good Friends and Brethren of the *Six Nations* had little

Reason to complain of any Injury from *Maryland*, and that they would be so well convinced thereof, on farther Deliberation, as he should hear no more of it; but you spoke of that Matter again to the Governor of *Pennsylvania*, about two Years since, as if you designed to terrify us.

IT was very inconsiderately said by you, that you would do yourselves Justice, by going to take Payment yourselves: Such an Attempt would have intirely dissolved the Chain of Friendship subsisting, not only between us, but perhaps the other *English* and you.

WE assure you, our People, who are numerous, courageous, and have Arms ready in their Hands, will not suffer themselves to be hurt in their Lives and Estates.

BUT, however, the old and wise People of *Maryland* immediately met in Council, and upon considering very coolly your rash Expressions, agreed to invite their Brethren, the *Six Nations*, to this Place, that they might learn of them what Right they have to the Land in *Maryland*, and, if they had any, to make them some reasonable Compensation for it; therefore the Governor of *Maryland* has sent us to meet and treat with you about this Affair, and the brightening and strengthening the Chain which hath long subsisted between us. And as an Earnest of our Sincerity and Good-will towards you, we present you with this Belt of Wampum.

On which the Indians *gave the* Yo-hah.

OUR *Great King of* ENGLAND, and his Subjects, have always possessed the Province of *Maryland* free and undisturbed from any Claim of the *Six Nations* for above one hundred Years past, and your not saying any thing to us before, convinces us you thought you had no Pretence to any Lands in *Maryland*; nor can we yet find out to what Lands, or under what Title, you make your Claim: For the *Sasquahannah* Indians, by a Treaty above ninety Years since (which is on the Table, and will be interpreted to you) give, and yield to the *English* Nation, their Heirs and Assigns for ever, the greatest Part (if not all) of the Lands we possess, from *Patuxent* River, on the Western, as well as from *Choptank* River, on the Eastern Side of the Great Bay of *Chessapeak*. And, near Sixty Years ago, you acknowledged to the Governor of *New-York* at *Albany*, "That you had given your Lands, and submitted yourselves to the King of *England*."[8]

---

[8]*"That you had given your Lands, and submitted yourselves to the King of England"*: What the Iroquois actually said in 1684 was less subservient than colonists claimed. An Onondaga did say, "We have put our Selves under the great Sachem Charles [King Charles II], that lives on the other side of the great Lake [the Atlantic Ocean].... We will not therefore joyn our selves or our Lands to any other Government but this." How-

WE are that Great King's Subjects, and we possess and enjoy the Province of *Maryland* by virtue of his Right and Sovereignty thereto; why, then, will you stir up any Quarrel between you and ourselves, who are as one Man, under the Protection of that Great King?

WE need not put you in mind of the Treaty (which we suppose you have had from your Fathers) made with the Province of *Maryland* near Seventy Years ago, and renewed and confirmed twice since that time.

BY these Treaties we became Brethren; we have always lived as such, and hope always to continue so.

WE have this further to say, that altho' we are not satisfied of the Justice of your Claim to any Lands in *Maryland*, yet we are desirous of shewing our Brotherly Kindness and Affection, and to prevent (by any reasonable Way) every Misunderstanding between the Province of *Maryland* and you our Brethren of the *Six Nations*.

FOR this Purpose we have brought hither a Quantity of Goods for our Brethren the *Six Nations*, and which will be delivered you as soon as we shall have received your Answer, and made so bright and large a Fire as may burn pure and clear whilst the Sun and Moon shall shine.

WE have now freely and openly laid our Bosoms bare to you; and that you may be the better confirmed of the Truth of our Hearts, we give you this Belt of Wampum.

Which was received with the Yo-Hah.

After a little Time Canassatego spoke as follows:

Brother, the Governor of Maryland,

WE have heard what you have said to us; and, as you have gone back to old Times, we cannot give you an Answer now, but shall take what you have said into Consideration, and return you our Answer some Time to Morrow. He then sat down, and after some Time he spoke again.

Brother, the Governor of Maryland,

IF you have made any Enquiry into *Indian* Affairs, you will know, that we have always had our Guns, Hatchets and Kettles, mended

---

ever, he went on to say, "Let your Friend, the great Sachem that lives on the other side the great Lake know this. We being a Free People, tho' united to the English, may give our Lands, and be joyn'd to the Sachem we like best." Later, another orator again made the Iroquois stance clear: "You say we are Subjects to the King of England . . . , but we say, we are Brethren." Francis Jennings, *The Ambiguous Iroquois Empire: The Covenant Chain Confederation of Indian Tribes with English Colonies from Its Beginnings to the Lancaster Treaty of 1744* (New York: W. W. Norton, 1984), 183.

when we came to see our Brethren. Brother *Onas*, and the Governor of *York* always do this for us; and we give you this early Notice, that we may not thereby be delayed, being desirous, as well as you, to give all possible Dispatch to the Business to be transacted between us.

THE Commissioners of *Virginia* and *Maryland* said, since it was customary, they would give Orders to have every Thing belonging to them mended that should want it.

In the COURT-HOUSE at *Lancaster, June* 26, 1744. *P. M.*

P R E S E N T,

The Honourable *GEORGE THOMAS*, Esq; Governor, &c.
The Honourable the Commissioners of *Virginia.*
The Honourable the Commissioners of *Maryland.*
The Deputies of the *Six Nations.*
Conrad Weiser, Interpreter.

CANASSATEGO spoke as follows:

Brother, the Governor of Maryland,

WHEN you invited us to kindle a Council Fire with you, *Conedogwainet*[9] was the Place agreed upon; but afterwards you, by Brother *Onas*, upon second Thoughts, considering that it would be difficult to get Provisions and other Accommodations where there were but few Houses or Inhabitants, desired we would meet our Brethren at *Lancaster*, and at his Instances we very readily agreed to meet you here, and are glad of the Change; for we have found Plenty of every thing; and as Yesterday you bid us welcome, and told us you were glad to see us, we likewise assure you we are as glad to see you; and, in Token of our Satisfaction, we present you with this String of Wampum.

Which was received with the usual Ceremony.

Brother, the Governor of Maryland,

YOU tell us, that when about Seven Years ago you heard, by our Brother *Onas*, of our Claim to some Lands in your Province, you took no Notice of it, believing, as you say, that when we should come to reconsider that Matter, we should find that we had no Right to make any Complaint of the Governor of *Maryland*, and would drop our

---

[9]*Conedogwainet* (Conodoguinet): An abandoned Indian town across the Susquehanna River from modern Harrisburg.

Demand. And that when about two Years ago we mentioned it again to our Brother *Onas*, you say we did it in such Terms as looked like a Design to terrify you; and you tell us further, that we must be beside ourselves, in using such a rash Expression as to tell you, We know how to do ourselves Justice if you still refuse. It is true we did say so, but without any ill Design; for we must inform you, that when we first desired our Brother *Onas* to use his Influence with you to procure us Satisfaction for our Lands, we, at the same time, desired him, in case you should disregard our Demand, to write to the Great King beyond the Seas, who would own us for his Children as well as you, to compel you to do us Justice: And, two Years ago, when we found that you had paid no Regard to our just Demand, nor that Brother *Onas* had convey'd our Complaint to the Great King over the Seas, we were resolved to use such Expressions as would make the greatest Impressions on your Minds, and we find it had its Effect; for you tell us, "That your wise Men held a Council together, and agreed to invite us, and to enquire of our Right to any of your Lands, and if it should be found that we had a Right, we were to have a Compensation made for them: And likewise you tell us, that our Brother, the Governor of *Maryland*, by the Advice of these wise Men, has sent you to brighten the Chain, and to assure us of his Willingness to remove whatever impedes a good Understanding between us." This shews that your wise Men understood our Expressions in their true Sense. We had no Design to terrify you, but to put you on doing us the Justice you had so long delayed. Your wise Men have done well; and as there is no Obstacle to a good Understanding between us, except this Affair of our Land, we, on our Parts, do give you the strongest Assurances of our good Dispositions towards you, and that we are as desirous as you to brighten the Chain, and to put away all Hindrances to a perfect good Understanding; and, in Token of our Sincerity, we give you this Belt of Wampum.

Which was received, and the Interpreter, ordered to give the Yo-Hah.

Brother, the Governor of Maryland,

WHEN you mentioned the Affair of the Land Yesterday, you went back to old Times, and told us, you had been in Possession of the Province of *Maryland* above One Hundred Years; but what is One Hundred Years in Comparison of the Length of Time since our Claim began? since we came out of this Ground? For we must tell you, that long before One Hundred Years our Ancestors came out of this very Ground, and their Children have remained here ever since. You came out of the Ground in a Country that lies beyond the Seas, there you may have a just Claim, but here you must allow us to be your elder Brethren, and the Lands to belong to us long before you knew any thing of them. It is true, that above One Hundred Years ago the *Dutch* came here in a Ship, and brought with them several Goods; such as Awls, Knives, Hatchets, Guns, and many other Particulars, which they gave us; and when they had taught us how to use their Things, and we saw what sort of People they were, we were so well pleased with them, that we tied their Ship to the Bushes on the Shore; and afterwards, liking them still better the longer they staid with us, and thinking the Bushes too slender, we removed the Rope, and tied it to the Trees; and as the Trees were liable to be blown down by high Winds, or to decay of themselves, we, from the Affection we bore them, again removed the Rope, and tied it to a strong and big Rock [*here the Interpreter said, They mean the* Oneido *Country*] and not content with this, for its further Security we removed the Rope to the big Mountain [*here the Interpreter says they mean the* Onandago *Country*] and there we tied it very fast, and rowll'd Wampum about it; and, to make it still more secure, we stood upon the Wampum, and sat down upon it, to defend it, and to prevent any Hurt coming to it, and did our best Endeavours that it might remain uninjured for ever. During all this Time the New-comers, the *Dutch*, acknowledged our Right to the Lands, and sollicited us, from Time to Time, to grant them Parts of our Country, and to enter into League and Covenant with us, and to become one People with us.

AFTER this the *English* came into the Country, and, as we were told, became one People with the *Dutch*. About two Years after the Arrival of the *English*, an *English* Governor came to *Albany*, and finding what great Friendship subsisted between us and the *Dutch*, he approved it mightily, and desired to make as strong a League, and to be upon as good Terms with us as the *Dutch* were, with whom he was united, and to become one People with us: And by his further Care in looking into what had passed between us, he found that the Rope which tied the Ship to the great Mountain was only fastened with Wampum, which was liable to break and rot, and to perish in a Course of Years; he therefore told us, he would give us a Silver Chain, which would be much stronger, and would last for ever. This we accepted, and fastened the Ship with it, and it has lasted ever since. Indeed we have had some small Differences with the *English*, and, during these Misunderstanding [*sic*], some of their young Men would, by way of Reproach, be every now and then telling us, that we should have perished if they had not come into the Country and furnished us with Strowds[10] and Hatchets, and Guns, and other Things necessary for the Support of Life; but we always gave them to understand that they were mistaken, that we lived before they came amongst us, and as well, or better, if we may believe what our Forefathers have told us. We had then Room enough, and Plenty of Deer, which was easily caught; and tho' we had not Knives, Hatchets, or Guns, such as we have now, yet we had Knives of Stone, and Hatchets of Stone, and Bows and Arrows, and those served our Uses as well then as the *English* ones do now. We are now straitened, and sometimes in want of Deer, and liable to many other Inconveniencies since the *English* came among us, and particularly from that Pen-and-Ink Work that is going on at the Table (*pointing to the Secretary*) and we will give you an Instance of this. Our Brother *Onas*, a great while ago, came to *Albany* to buy the *Sasquahannah* Lands of us, but our Brother, the Governor of *New-York*, who, as we suppose, had not a good Understanding with our Brother *Onas*, advised us not to sell him any Land, for he would make an ill Use of it; and, pretending to be our good Friend, he advised us, in order to prevent *Onas*'s, or any other Person's imposing upon us, and that we might always have our Land when we should want it, to put it into his Hands; and told us, he would keep it for our Use, and never open his Hands, but keep them close shut, and not part with any of it, but at our Request. Accordingly we trusted him, and put our Land into his Hands, and charged him to keep it safe for our Use; but, some Time after, he went to *England*, and carried our Land with him, and there sold it to our Brother *Onas* for a large Sum of Money; and when, at the Instance of our Brother *Onas*, we were minded to sell him some Lands, he told us, we had sold the *Sasquahannah* Lands already to the Governor of *New-York*, and that he had bought them from him in *England*; tho', when he came to understand how the Governor of *New-York* had deceived us, he very generously paid us for our Lands over again.

THO' we mention this Instance of an Imposition put upon us by the Governor of *New-York*, yet we must do the *English* the Justice to say, we have had their hearty Assistances in our Wars with the *French*, who were no sooner arrived amongst us than they began to render us uneasy, and to provoke us to War, and we have had several Wars with them; during all which we constantly received Assistance from the

---

[10] *Strowds* (strouds): Blankets made in Britain particularly for the Indian trade.

English, and, by their Means, we have always been able to keep up our Heads against their Attacks.

WE now come nearer home. We have had your Deeds interpreted to us, and we acknowledge them to be good and valid, and that the *Conestogoe* or *Sasquahannah Indians* had a Right to sell those Lands to you, for they were then theirs; but since that Time we have conquered them, and their Country now belongs to us, and the Lands we demanded Satisfaction for are no Part of the Lands comprized in those Deeds; they are the *Cohongorontas* Lands; those, we are sure, you have not possessed One Hundred Years, no, nor above Ten Years, and we made our Demands so soon as we knew your People were settled in those Parts. These have never been sold, but remain still to be disposed of; and we are well pleased to hear you are provided with Goods, and do assure you of our Willingness to treat with you for those unpurchased Lands; in Confirmation whereof, we present you with this Belt of Wampum.

Which was received with the usual Ceremonies.

CANASSATEGO added, that as the three Governors of *Virginia, Maryland,* and *Pennsylvania,* had divided the Lands among them, they could not, for this Reason, tell how much each had got, nor were they concerned about it, so that they were paid by all the Governors for the Several Parts each possessed, and this they left to their Honour and Justice.

In the COURT-HOUSE at *Lancaster, June* 27, 1744, *A. M.*

P R E S E N T,

The Honourable *GEORGE THOMAS*, Esq; Governor, &c.
The Honourable the Commissioners of *Virginia*.
The Honourable the Commissioners of *Maryland*.
The Deputies of the *Six Nations*.
Conrad Weiser, Interpreter.

The Commissioners of Virginia *ordered the Interpreter to let the* Indians *know the Governor of* Virginia *was going to speak to them, and then they spoke as follows:*

Sachims and Warriors of the Six United Nations, *our Friends and Brethren,*

* *Cohongorontas*, i. e. *Potomack.* [Franklin note.]

A T our Desire the Governor of *Pennsylvania* invited you to this Conncil [*sic*] Fire; we have waited a long Time for you, but now you are come, you are heartily welcome; we are very glad to see you; we give you this String of Wampum.

Which was received with their usual Approbation.

Brethren,

IN the Year 1736, four of your Sachims wrote a Letter to *James Logan*, Esq; then President of *Pennsylvania*,[11] to let the Governor of *Virginia* know that you expected some Consideration for Lands in the Occupation of some of the People of *Virginia*. Upon seeing a Copy of this Letter, the Governor, with the Council of *Virginia*, took some Time to consider of it. They found, on looking into the old Treaties, that you had given up your Lands to the Great King, who has had Possession of *Virginia* above One Hundred and Sixty Years, and under that Great King the Inhabitants of *Virginia* hold their Land, so they thought there might be some Mistake.

WHEREFORE they desired the Governor of *New-York* to enquire of you about it. He sent his Interpreter to you in *May*, 1743, who laid this before you at a Council held at *Onandago*, to which you answer, "That if you had any Demand or Pretensions on the Governor of *Virginia* any way, you would have made it known to the Governor of *New-York*." This corresponds with what you have said to Governor *Thomas*, in the Treaty made with him at *Philadelphia* in *July*, 1742; for then you only make your Claim to Lands in the Government of *Maryland*.

WE are so well pleased with this good Faith of you our Brethren of the *Six Nations*, and your Regard to the Treaties made with *Virginia*, that we are ready to hear you on the Subject of your Message eight Years since.

TELL us what Nations of *Indians* you conquered any Lands from in *Virginia*, how long it is since, and what Possession you have had; and if it does appear, that there is any Land on the Borders of *Virginia* that the *Six Nations* have a Right to, we are willing to make you Satisfaction.

Then laid down a String of Wampum, which was accepted with the usual Ceremony, and then added,

WE have a Chest of new Goods, and the Key is in our Pockets. You are our Brethren; the Great King is our common Father, and we will live with you, as Children ought to do, in Peace and Love.

---

[11] *President of Pennsylvania*: The head of the Pennsylvania Provincial Council.

WE will brighten the Chain, and strengthen the Union between us; so that we shall never be divided, but remain Friends and Brethren as long as the Sun gives Light; in Confirmation whereof, we give you this Belt of Wampum.

Which was received with the usual Ceremony.

TACHANOONTIA replied:

Brother Assaragoa,

YOU have made a good Speech to us, which is very agreeable, and for which we return you our Thanks. We shall be able to give you an Answer to every Part of it some Time this Afternoon, and we will let you know when we are ready.

In the COURT-HOUSE at *Lancaster, June* 27, 1744. *P. M.*

PRESENT,

The Honourable *GEORGE THOMAS*, Esq; Governor, &c.
The Honourable the Commissioners of *Virginia.*
The Honourable the Commissioners of *Maryland.*
The Deputies of the *Six Nations.*
Conrad Weiser, Interpreter.

TACHANOONTIA spoke as follows:

Brother Assaragoa,

SINCE you have joined with the Governor of *Maryland* and Brother *Onas* in kindling this Fire, we gladly acknowledge the Pleasure we have in seeing you here, and observing your good Dispositions as well to confirm the Treaties of Friendship, as to enter into further Contracts about Land with us; and, in Token of our Satisfaction, we present you with this String of Wampum.

Which was received with the usual Ceremonies.

Brother Assaragoa,

IN your Speech this Morning you were pleased to say we had wrote a Letter to *James Logan*, about seven Years ago, to demand a Consideration for our Lands in the Possession of some of the *Virginians*; that you held them under the Great King for upwards of One Hundred and Sixty Years, and that we had already given up our Right; and that therefore you had desired the Governor of *New-York* to send his Interpreter to us last Year to *Onandago*, which he did; and, as you say, we in Council at *Onandago* did declare, that we had no Demand upon you for Lands, and that if we had any Pretensions, we should have made them known to the Governor of *New-York*; and likewise you desire to know if we have any Right to the *Virginia* Lands, and that we will make such Right appear, and tell you what Nations of *Indians* we conquered those Lands from.

Now we answer, We have the Right of Conquest, a Right too dearly purchased, and which cost us too much Blood, to give up without any Reason at all, as you say we have done at *Albany*; but we should be obliged to you, if you would let us see the Letter, and inform us who was the Interpreter, and whose Names are put to that Letter; for as the whole Transaction cannot be above a Year's standing, it must be fresh in every Body's Memory, and some of our Council would easily remember it; but we assure you, and are well able to prove, that neither we, nor any Part of us, have ever relinquished our Right, or ever gave such an Answer as you say is mentioned in your Letter. Could we, so few Years ago, make a formal Demand, by *James Logan*, and not be sensible of our Right? And hath any thing happened since that Time to make us less sensible? No; and as this Matter can be easily cleared up, we are anxious it should be done; for we are positive no such thing was ever mentioned to us at *Onandago*, nor any where else. All the World knows we conquered the several Nations living on *Sasquahanna*, *Cohongoronta*, and on the Back of the Great Mountains in *Virginia*; the *Conoy-uch-such-roona*, *Coch-now-was-roonan*, *Tohoa-irough-roonan*, and *Connutskin-ough-roonaw*,[12] feel the Effects of our Conquests, being now a Part of our Nations, and their Lands at our Disposal. We know very well, it hath often been said by the *Virginians*, that the *Great King of* ENGLAND, and the People of that Colony, conquered the *Indians* who lived there, but it is not true. We will allow they have conquered the *Sachdagughroonaw*,[13] and drove back the

---

[12] *Conoy-uch-such-roona*: The Conoys, who lived along the Potomac River in what is now Maryland before moving north around 1700 to the Susquehanna River Valley under Iroquois protection. *Coch-now-was-roonan*: Kanawa, from the Potomac's headwaters (the modern Kanawa River is in West Virginia). *Tohoa-irough-roonan*: Tutelos, Siouan-speaking people from the southern piedmont who moved to the Susquehanna Valley in the early eighteenth century. *Connutskin-ough-roonaw*: "House-corner people" (unknown). *Roonan, roonaw, roona* was an Iroquois suffix meaning "people." William N. Fenton, *The Great Law and the Longhouse: A Political History of the Iroquois Confederacy* (Norman: University of Oklahoma Press, 1998), 428.

[13] *Sachdagughroonaw*: Perhaps the Powhatan peoples of the Tidewater region of Virginia, where more than a century before Capt. John Smith reported a town called *Sekacawone* (or "Secacawoni"). William C. Sturtevant, gen. ed., *Handbook of North American Indians*, vol. 15, *Northeast*, ed. Bruce G. Trigger (Washington, D.C.: Smithsonian Institution, 1978), 269.

Tuscarroraws, and that they have, on that Account, a Right to some Part of *Virginia*; but as to what lies beyond the Mountains, we conquered the Nations residing there, and that Land, if the *Virginians* ever get a good Right to it, it must be by us; and in Testimony of the Truth of our Answer to this Part of your Speech, we give you this String of Wampum.

Which was received with the usual Ceremony.

Brother Assaragoa,

WE have given you a full Answer to the first Part of your Speech, which we hope will be satisfactory. We are glad to hear you have brought with you a big Chest of new Goods, and that you have the Key in your Pockets. We do not doubt but we shall have a good Understanding in all Points, and come to an Agreement with you.

WE shall open all our Hearts to you, that you may know every thing in them; we will hide nothing from you; and we hope, if there be any thing still remaining in your Breast that may occasion any Dispute between us, you will take the Opportunity to unbosom your Hearts, and lay them open to us, that henceforth there may be no Dirt, nor any other Obstacle in the Road between us; and in Token of our hearty Wishes to bring about so good an Harmony, we present you with this Belt of Wampum.

Which was received with the usual Ceremony.

Brother Assaragoa,

WE must now tell you what Mountains we mean that we say are the Boundaries between you and us. You may remember, that about twenty Years ago you had a Treaty with us at *Albany*, when you took a Belt of Wampum, and made a Fence with it on the Middle of the Hill, and told us, that if any of the Warriors of the *Six Nations* came on your Side of the Middle of the Hill, you would hang them; and you gave us Liberty to do the same with any of your People who should be found on our Side of the Middle of the Hill. This is the Hill we mean, and we desire that Treaty may be now confirmed. After we left *Albany*, we brought our Road a great deal more to the West, that we might comply with your Proposal; but, tho' it was of your own making, your People never observed it, but came and lived on our Side of the Hill, which we don't blame you for, as you live at a great Distance, near the Seas, and cannot be thought to know what your People do in the Backparts: And on their settling, contrary to your own Proposal, on our new Road, it fell out that our Warriors did some Hurt to your People's Cattle, of which a Complaint was made, and transmitted to us by our

Brother *Onas*; and we, at his Request, altered the Road again, and brought it to the Foot of the Great Mountain, where it now is; and it is impossible for us to remove it any further to the West, those Parts of the Country being absolutely impassable by either Man or Beast.

WE had not been long in the Use of this new Road before your People came, like Flocks of Birds, and sat down on both Sides of it, and yet we never made a Complaint to you, tho' you must be sensible those Things must have been done by your People in manifest Breach of your own Proposal made at *Albany*; and therefore, as we are now opening our Hearts to you, we cannot avoid complaining, and desire all these Affairs may be settled, and that you may be stronger induced to do us Justice for what is past, and to come to a thorough Settlement for the future, we, in the Presence of the Governor of *Maryland*, and Brother *Onas*, present you with this Belt of Wampum.

Which was received with the usual Ceremony.

Then Tachanoontia *added*:

HE forgot to say, that the Affair of the Road must be looked upon as a Preliminary to be settled before the Grant of Lands; and that either the *Virginia* People must be obliged to remove more Easterly, or, if they are permitted to stay, that our Warriors, marching that Way to the Southward, shall go Sharers with them in what they plant.

In the COURT-HOUSE at *Lancaster, June* 28, 1744, *A. M.*

PRESENT,

The Honourable *GEORGE THOMAS*, Esq; Governor, &c.
The Honourable the Commissioners of *Virginia*.
The Honourable the Commissioners of *Maryland*.
The Deputies of the *Six Nations*.
Conrad Weiser, Interpreter.

The GOVERNOR *spoke as follows:*

Friends and Brethren of the Six Nations,

I AM always sorry when any thing happens that may create the least Uneasiness between us; but as we are mutually engaged to keep the Road between us clear and open, and to remove every Obstruction that may lie in the Way, I must inform you, that three of the *Delaware Indians* lately murdered *John Armstrong*, an *Indian* Trader, and his two Men, in a most barbarous Manner, as he was travelling to *Allegheny*, and stole his Goods of a considerable Value. *Shick Calamy*, and the *Indians* settled at *Shamokin*,[14] did well; they seized two of the Murderers, and sent them down to our Settlements; but the *Indians*, who had the Charge of them, afterwards suffered one of them to escape, on a Pretence that he was not concerned in the bloody Deed; the other is now in *Philadelphia* Goal.[15] By our Law all the Accessaries to a Murder are to be tried, and put to Death, as well as the Person who gave the deadly Wound. If they consented to it, encouraged it, or any ways assisted in it, they are to be put to Death, and it is just it should be so. If, upon Trial, the Persons present at the Murder are found not to have done any of these Things, they are set at Liberty. Two of our People were, not many Years ago, publickly put to Death for killing two *Indians*; we therefore expect you will take the most effectual Measures to seize and deliver up to us the other two *Indians* present at these Murders, to be tried with the Principal now in Custody. If it shall appear, upon their Trial, that they were not advising, or any way assisting in this horrid Fact, they will be acquitted, and sent home to their Towns. And that you may be satisfied no Injustice will be done to them, I do now invite you to depute three or four *Indians* to be present at their Trials. I do likewise expect that you will order strict Search to be made for the Remainder of the stolen Goods, that they may be restored to the Wife and Children of the Deceased. That what I have said may have its due Weight with you, I give you this String of Wampum.

Which was accepted with the Yo-hah.

THE Governor afterwards ordered the Interpreter to tell them, he expected a very full Answer from them, and that they might take their own Time to give it; for he did not desire to interfere with the Business of *Virginia* and *Maryland*.

THEY said they would take it into Consideration, and give a full Answer.

THEN the Commissioners of *Virginia* let them know, by the Interpreter, that they would speak to them in the Afternoon.

---

[14] *Shamokin*: A major Indian town (inhabited by Iroquois, Delawares, Shawnees, and other native groups) at the junction of the Susquehanna River's two branches.
[15] *Goal*: Jail.

In the CourT-House Chamber at *Lancaster, June* 28, 1744, *P. M.*

P R E S E N T ,

The Honourable the Commissioners of *Maryland.*
The Deputies of the *Six Nations.*
Conrad Weiser, Interpreter.

The Commissioners desired the Interpreter to tell the Indians *they were going to speak to them. Mr.* Weiser *acquainted them herewith. After which the said Commissioners spoke as follows:*

Our good Friends and Brethren, the Six *united* Nations,

W E have considered what you said concerning your Title to some Lands now in our Province, and also of the Place where they lie. Altho' we cannot admit your Right, yet we are so resolved to live in Brotherly Love and Affection with the *Six Nations*, that upon your giving us a Release in Writing of all your Claim to any Lands in *Maryland*, we shall make you a Compensation to the Value of Three Hundred Pounds Currency,[16] for the Payment of Part whereof we have brought some Goods, and shall make up the rest in what Manner you think fit.

As we intend to say something to you about our Chain of Friendship after this Affair of the Land is settled, we desire you will now examine the Goods, and make an End of this Matter.

We will not omit acquainting our good Friends the *Six Nations*, that notwithstanding we are likely to come to an Agreement about your Claim of Lands, yet your Brethren of *Maryland* look on you to be as one Soul and one Body with themselves; and as a broad Road will be made between us, we shall always be desirous of keeping it clear, that we may, from Time to Time, take care that the Links of our Friendship be not rusted. In Testimony that our Words and our Hearts agree, we give you this Belt of Wampum.

On presenting of which the Indians *gave the usual Cry of Approbation.*

Mr. *Weiser* acquainted the *Indians*, they might now look over the several Goods placed on a Table in the Chamber for that Purpose; and the honourable Commissioners bid him tell them, if they disliked any

---

[16] *Currency:* Pennsylvania paper money, of less value than gold or British sterling.

of the Goods, or, if they were damaged, the Commissioners would put a less Price on such as were either disliked or damnified.

THE *Indians* having viewed and examined the Goods, and seeming dissatisfied at the Price and Worth of them, required Time to go down into the Court-House, in order for a Consultation to be had by the Chiefs of them concerning the said Goods, and likewise that the Interpreter might retire with them, which he did. Accordingly they went down into the Court-House, and soon after returned again into the Chamber.

MR. *Weiser* sat down among the *Indians*, and discoursed them about the Goods, and in some short Time after they chose the following from among the others, and the Price agreed to be given for them by the *Six Nations* was, *viz.*

	£.	s.	d.
Four Pieces of Strowds, at 7 £.	28	00	00
Two Pieces Ditto, 5 £.	10	00	00
Two Hundred Shirts,	63	12	00
Three Pieces Half-Thicks,[17]	11	00	00
Three Pieces Duffle[18] Blankets, at 7 £.	21	00	00
One Piece Ditto,	6	10	00
Forty Seven Guns, at 1 £. 6 s.	61	2	00
One Pound Vermillion,[19]	00	18	00
One Thousand Flints,	00	18	00
Four Dozen Jews Harps,[20]	00	14	00
One Dozen Boxes,	00	1	00
One Hundred Two Quarters Bar-Lead,	3	00	00
Two Quarters Shot,	1	00	00
Two Half-Barrels of Gun-Powder,	13	00	00
£.	220	15	00

Pennsylvania Currency.

WHEN the *Indians* had agreed to take these Goods at the Rates above specified, they informed the Interpreter, that they would give an Answer to the Speech made to them this Morning by the honourable the Commissioners of *Maryland*, but did not express the Time when

---

[17] *Half-Thicks*: A coarse cloth.
[18] *Duffle*: A coarse cloth.
[19] *Vermillion*: A red paint.
[20] *Jews Harps*: Small metal musical instruments played with the hands and mouth; Indians probably fashioned these into tools or decorative items.

such Answer should be made. At 12 o'Clock the Commissioners departed the Chamber.

In the COURT-HOUSE at *Lancaster, June* 28, 1744, *P. M.*

The Honourable *GEORGE THOMAS*, Esq; Governor, &c.
The Honourable the Commissioners of *Virginia.*
The Honourable the Commissioners of *Maryland.*
The Deputies of the *Six Nations.*
Conrad Weiser, Interpreter.

The Commissioners of Virginia *desired the Interpreter to let the*
Indians *know, that their Brother* Assaragoa *was now going to give his*
Reply to their Answer to his first Speech, delivered them the Day
before in the Forenoon.

Sachims and Warriors of the united Six Nations,

W E are now come to answer what you said to us Yesterday, since
what we said to you before on the Part of the Great King, our
Father, has not been satisfactory. You have gone into old Times, and
so must we. It is true that the Great King holds *Virginia* by Right of
Conquest, and the Bounds of that Conquest to the Westward is the
Great Sea.

IF the *Six Nations* have made any Conquest over *Indians* that may
at any Time have lived on the West-side of the Great Mountains of *Virginia*, yet they never possessed any Lands there that we have ever
heard of. That Part was altogether deserted, and free for any People to
enter upon, as the People of *Virginia* have done, by Order of the Great
King, very justly, as well by an ancient Right, as by its being freed
from the Possession of any other, and from any Claim even of you the
Six Nations, our Brethren, until within these eight Years. The first
Treaty between the Great King, in Behalf of his Subjects of *Virginia*,
and you, that we can find, was made at *Albany*, by Colonel *Henry*
Coursey, Seventy Years since; this was a Treaty of Friendship, when the
first Covenant Chain was made, when we and you became Brethren.

THE next Treaty was also at *Albany*, above Fifty-eight Years ago, by
the Lord *Howard*, Governor of *Virginia*; then you declare yourselves
Subjects to the Great King, our Father, and gave up to him all your
Lands for his Protection. This you own[21] in a Treaty made by the Governor of *New-York* with you at the same Place in the Year 1687, and

---

[21] *own*: Admit, acknowledge.

you express yourselves in these Words, "Brethren, you tell us the King of *England* is a very great King, and why should not you join with us in a very just Cause, when the *French* join with our Enemies in an unjust Cause? O Brethren, we see the Reason of this; for the *French* would fain kill us all, and when that is done, they would carry all the Beaver Trade to *Canada*, and the *Great King of* ENGLAND would lose the Land likewise; and therefore, O Great Sachim, beyond the Great Lakes, awake, and suffer not those poor *Indians*, that have given themselves and their Lands under your Protection, to be destroyed by the *French* without a Cause."

THE last Treaty we shall speak to you about is that made at *Albany* [in 1722] by Governor *Spotswood*, which you have not recited as it is: For the white People, your Brethren of *Virginia*, are, in no Article of that Treaty, prohibited to pass, and settle to the Westward of the Great Mountains. It is the *Indians*, tributary to *Virginia*, that are restrained, as you and your tributary *Indians* are from passing to the Eastward of the same Mountains, or to the Southward of *Cohongorooton*, and you agree to this Article in these Words; "That the Great River of *Potowmack*, and the high Ridge of Mountains, which extend all along the Frontiers of *Virginia* to the Westward of the present Settlements of that Colony, shall be for ever the established Boundaries between the *Indians* subject to the Dominions of *Virginia*, and the *Indians* belonging and depending on the *Five Nations*; so that neither our *Indians* shall not, on any Pretence whatsoever, pass to Northward or Westward of the said Boundaries, without having to produce a Passport under the Hand and Seal of the Governor or Commander in Chief of *Virginia*; nor your *Indians* to pass to the Southward or Eastward of the said Boundaries, without a Passport in like Manner from the Governor or Commander in Chief of *New-York*."

AND what Right can you have to Lands that you have no Right to walk upon, but upon certain Conditions? It is true, you have not observed this Part of the Treaty, and your Brethren of *Virginia* have not insisted upon it with a due Strictness, which has occasioned some Mischief.

THIS Treaty has been sent to the Governor of *Virginia* by Order of the Great King, and is what we must rely on, and, being in Writing, is more certain than your Memory. That is the Way the white People have of preserving Transactions of every Kind, and transmitting them down to their Childrens Children for ever, and all Disputes among them are settled by this faithful kind of Evidence, and must be the Rule between the Great King and you. This Treaty your Sachims and

Warriors signed some Years after the same Governor *Spotswood*, in the Right of the Great King, had been, with some People of *Virginia*, in Possession of these very Lands, which you have set up your late Claim to.

THE Commissioners for *Indian* Affairs at *Albany* gave the Account we mentioned to you Yesterday to the Governor of *New-York*, and he sent it to the Governor of *Virginia*; their Names will be given you by the Interpreter.

Brethren,

THIS Dispute is not between *Virginia* and you; it is setting up your Right against the Great King, under whose Grants the People you complain of are settled. Nothing but a Command from the Great King can remove them; they are too powerful to be removed by any Force of you, our Brethren; and the Great King, as our Common Father, will do equal Justice to all his Children; wherefore we do believe they will be confirmed in their Possessions.

As to the Road you mention, we intended to prevent any Occasion for it, by making a Peace between you and the Southern *Indians*, a few Years since, at a considerable Expence to our Great King, which you confirmed at *Albany*. It seems, by your being at War with the *Catawbas*, that it has not been long kept between you.

HOWEVER, if you desire a Road, we will agree to one on the Terms of the Treaty you made with Colonel *Spotswood*, and your People, behaving themselves orderly like Friends and Brethren, shall be used in their Passage through *Virginia* with the same Kindness as they are when they pass through the Lands of your Brother *Onas*. This, we hope, will be agreed to by you our Brethren, and we will abide by the Promise made to you Yesterday.

WE may proceed to settle what we are to give you for any Right you may have, or have had to all the Lands to the Southward and Westward of the Lands of your Brother the Governor of *Maryland*, and of your Brother *Onas*; tho' we are informed that the Southern *Indians* claim these very Lands that you do.

WE are desirous to live with you, our Brethren, according to the old Chain of Friendship, to settle all these Matters fairly and honestly; and, as a Pledge of our Sincerity, we give you this Belt of Wampum.

Which was received with the usual Ceremony.

In the COURT-HOUSE Chamber at *Lancaster, June* 29, 1744, *A. M.*

PRESENT,

The Honourable the Commissioners of *Maryland.*
The Deputies of the *Six Nations.*
Conrad Weiser, Interpreter.

Mr. Weiser *informed the honourable Commissioners, the* Indians *were ready to give their Answer to the Speech made to them here Yesterday Morning by the Commissioners; whereupon* Canassatego *spoke as follows, looking on a Deal-board,*[22] *where were some black Lines, describing the Courses of* Potowmack *and* Sasquahanna:
Brethren,

YESTERDAY you spoke to us concerning the Lands on this Side *Potowmack* River, and as we have deliberately considered what you said to us on that Matter, we are now very ready to settle the Bounds of such Lands, and release our Right and Claim thereto.

WE are willing to renounce all Right to Lord *Baltimore*[23] of all those Lands lying two Miles above the uppermost Fork of *Potowmack* or *Cohongoruton* River, near which *Thomas Cressap*[24] has a hunting or trading Cabin, by a North-line, to the Bounds of *Pennsylvania.* But in case such Limits shall not include every Settlement or Inhabitant of *Maryland,* then such other Lines and Courses, from the said two Miles above the Forks, to the outermost Inhabitants or Settlements, as shall include every Settlement and Inhabitant in *Maryland,* and from thence, by a North-line, to the Bounds of *Pennsylvania,* shall be the Limits. And further, If any People already have, or shall settle beyond the Lands now described and bounded, they shall enjoy the same free from any Disturbance whatever, and we do, and shall accept these People for our Brethren, and as such always treat them.

WE earnestly desire to live with you as Brethren, and hope you will shew us all Brotherly Kindness; in Token whereof, we present you with a Belt of Wampum.

Which was received with the usual Ceremony.

---

[22] *Deal-board*: A board made of pine or fir.
[23] *Lord Baltimore*: Proprietor of the colony of Maryland.
[24] *Thomas Cressap* (c. 1702–c. 1790): A fur trader who lived on the Maryland frontier near the upper Potomac River.

SOON after the Commissioners and *Indians* departed from the Court-House Chamber.

In the COURT-HOUSE Chamber at *Lancaster, June* 30, 1744, *A. M.*

P R E S E N T ,

The Honourable the Commissioners of *Virginia.*
The Deputies of the *Six Nations.*
Conrad Weiser, Interpreter.

Gachradodow, *Speaker for the* Indians, *in Answer to the Commissioners Speech at the last Meeting, with a strong Voice, and proper Action, spoke as follows:*

Brother Assaragoa,

THE World at the first was made on the other Side of the Great Water different from what it is on this Side, as may be known from the different Colours of our Skin, and of our Flesh, and that which you call Justice may not be so amongst us; you have your Laws and Customs, and so have we. The Great King might send you over to conquer the *Indians*, but it looks to us that God did not approve of it; if he had, he would not have placed the Sea where it is, as the Limits between us and you.

Brother Assaragoa,

THO' great Things are well remembered among us, yet we don't remember that we were ever conquered by the Great King, or that we have been employed by that Great King to conquer others; if it was so, it is beyond our Memory. We do remember we were employed by *Maryland* to conquer the *Conestogoes*, and that the second time we were at War with them, we carried them all off.

Brother Assaragoa,

YOU charge us with not acting agreeable to our Peace with the *Catawbas*, we will repeat to you truly what was done. The Governor of *New-York*, at *Albany*, in Behalf of *Assaragoa*, gave us several Belts of Wampum from the *Cherikees* and *Catawbas*, and we agreed to a Peace, if those Nations would send some of their great Men to us to confirm it Face to Face, and that they would trade with us; and desired that they would appoint a Time to meet at *Albany* for that Purpose, but they never came.

Brother Assaragoa,

WE then desired a Letter might be sent to the *Catawbas* and *Cherikees*, to desire them to come and confirm the Peace. It was long before an Answer came; but we met the *Cherikees*, and confirmed the Peace, and sent some of our People to take care of them, until they returned to their own Country.

THE *Catawbas* refused to come, and sent us word, That we were but Women, that they were Men, and double Men, for they had two P———s;[25] that they could make Women of us, and would be always at War with us. They are a deceitful People. Our Brother *Assaragoa* is deceived by them; we don't blame him for it, but are sorry he is so deceived.

Brother Assaragoa,

WE have confirmed the Peace with the *Cherikees*, but not with the *Catawbas*. They have been treacherous, and know it; so that the War must continue till one of us is destroyed. This we think proper to tell you, that you may not be troubled at what we do to the *Catawbas*.

Brother Assaragoa,

WE will now speak to the Point between us. You say you will agree with us as to the Road; we desire that may be the Road which was last made (the Waggon-Road.) It is always a Custom among Brethren or Strangers to use each other kindly; you have some very ill-natured People living up there; so that we desire the Persons in Power may know that we are to have reasonable Victuals when we are in want.

YOU know very well, when the white People came first here they were poor; but now they have got our Lands, and are by them become rich, and we are now poor; what little we have had for the Land goes soon away, but the Land lasts for ever. You told us you had brought with you a Chest of Goods, and that you have the Key in your Pockets; but we have never seen the Chest, nor the Goods that are said to be in it; it may be small, and the Goods few; we want to see them, and are desirous to come to some Conclusion. We have been sleeping here these ten Days past, and have not done any thing to the Purpose.

THE Commissioners told them they should see the Goods on *Monday.*

---

[25]The Williamsburg edition of this treaty offers, in a footnote, the following explanation of this metaphor: "This is a Figure by which the *Indians* express Strength and Power. So when the Governor of *Canada* designs to explain to the *Indians* the Power and Strength of the grand Monarch, he tells them his *P———k* is as large as he can span with both his Hands." *The Treaty Held with the* Indians *of the Six Nations, At* Lancaster, *in* Pennsylvania, *in* June, *1744 . . .* (Williamsburg: William Parks, 1744), 43.

In the Court-House at *Lancaster, June* 30, 1744, *P. M.*

P R E S E N T,

The Honourable *GEORGE THOMAS*, Esq; Governor, &c.
The Honourable the Commissioners of *Virginia.*
The Honourable the Commissioners of *Maryland.*
The Deputies of the *Six Nations.*
Conrad Weiser, Interpreter.

THE three Governments entertained the *Indians*, and all the Gentlemen in Town, with a handsome Dinner. The *Six Nations*, in their Order, having returned Thanks with the usual Solemnity of *Yo-ha-han*, the Interpreter informed the Governor and the Commissioners, that as the Lord Proprietor and Governor of *Maryland* was not known to the *Indians* by any particular Name, they had agreed, in Council, to take the first Opportunity of a large Company to present him with one; and as this with them is deemed a Matter of great Consequence, and attended with Abundance of Form, the several Nations had drawn Lots for the Performance of the Ceremony, and the Lot falling on the *Cayogo* Nation, they had chosen *Gachradodow*, one of their Chiefs, to be their Speaker, and he desired Leave to begin; which being given, he, on an elevated Part of the Court-House, with all the Dignity of a Warrior, the Gesture of an Orator, and in a very graceful Posture, spoke as follows:

"As the Governor of *Maryland* had invited them here to treat about their Lands, and brighten the Chain of Friendship, the united Nations thought themselves so much obliged to them, that they had come to a Resolution in Council to give to the great Man, who is Proprietor of *Maryland*, a particular Name, by which they might hereafter correspond with him; and as it had fallen to the *Cayogoes* Lot in Council to consider of a proper Name for the chief Man, they had agreed to give him the Name of *Tocarry-hogan*, denoting Precedency, Excellency, or living in the middle or honourable Place betwixt *Assaragoa* and their Brother *Onas*, by whom their Treaties might be better carried on." And then, addressing himself to his Honour the Governor of *Pennsylvania*, the honourable the Commissioners of *Virginia* and *Maryland*, and to the Gentlemen then present, he proceeded:

"As there is a Company of great Men now assembled, we take this Time and Opportunity to publish this Matter, that it may be known

Tocarry-hogan is our Friend, and that we are ready to honour him, and that by such Name he may be always called and known among us. And we hope he will ever act towards us according to the Excellency of the Name we have now given him, and enjoy a long and happy Life."

THE honourable the Governor and Commissioners, and all the Company present, returned the Compliment with three Huzza's, and, after drinking Healths to our gracious King and the *Six Nations*, the Commissioners of *Maryland* proceeded to Business in the Court-House Chamber with the *Indians*, where *Conrad Weiser*, the Interpreter, was present.

THE honourable the Commissioners ordered Mr. *Weiser* to tell the *Indians*, that a Deed, releasing all their Claim and Title to certain Lands lying in the Province of *Maryland*, which by them was agreed to be given and executed for the Use of the Lord Baron of *Baltimore*, Lord Proprietary of that Province, was now on the Table, and Seals ready fixed thereto. The Interpreter acquainted them therewith as desired, and then gave the Deed to *Canassatego*, the Speaker, who made his Mark, and put his Seal, and delivered it; after which, thirteen other Chiefs or Sachims of the *Six Nations* executed it in the same Manner, in the Presence of the honourable the Commissioners of *Virginia*, and divers other Gentlemen of that Colony, and of the Provinces of *Pennsylvania* and *Maryland*.

At the House of Mr. *George Sanderson* in *Lancaster*,
July 2, 1744, *A. M.*

P R E S E N T,

The Honourable the Commissioners of *Maryland*.
The Deputies of the *Six Nations*.
Conrad Weiser, Interpreter.

THE several Chiefs of the *Indians* of the *Six Nations*, who had not signed the Deed of Release of their Claim to some Lands in *Maryland*, tendered to them on Saturday last, in the Chamber of the Court-House in this Town, did now readily execute the same, and caused Mr. *Weiser* likewise to sign it, as well with his *Indian*, as with his own proper Name of *Weiser*, as a Witness and Interpreter.

In the Court-House at *Lancaster, July* 2, 1744. *A. M.*

P R E S E N T,

The Honourable *GEORGE THOMAS*, Esq; Governor, &c.
The Honourable the Commissioners of *Virginia*.
The Honourable the Commissioners of *Maryland*.
The Deputies of the *Six Nations*.
Conrad Weiser, Interpreter.

CANASSATEGO spoke as follows:

Brother Onas,

THE other Day you was pleased to tell us, you were always concerned whenever any thing happened that might give you or us Uneasiness, and that we were mutually engaged to preserve the Road open and clear between us; and you informed us of the Murder of *John Armstrong*, and his two Men, by some of the *Delaware Indians*, and of their stealing his Goods to a considerable Value. The *Delaware Indians*, as you suppose, are under our Power. We join with you in your Concern for such a vile Proceeding; and, to testify that we have the same Inclinations with you to keep the Road clear, free and open, we give you this String of Wampum.

Which was received with the usual Ceremony.

Brother Onas,

THESE Things happen frequently, and we desire you will consider them well, and not be too much concerned. Three *Indians* have been killed at different Times at *Ohio*, and we never mentioned any of them to you, imagining it might have been occasioned by some unfortunate Quarrels, and being unwilling to create a Disturbance. We therefore desire you will consider these Things well, and, to take the Grief from your Heart, we give you this String of Wampum.

Which was received with the usual Ceremonies.

Brother Onas,

WE had heard of the Murder of *John Armstrong*, and, in our Journey here, we had Conference with our Cousins the *Delawares* about it, and reproved them severely for it, and charged them to go down to our Brother *Onas*, and make him Satisfaction, both for the Men that were killed, and for the Goods. We understood, by them, that the principal Actor in these Murders is in your Prison, and that he had done all the Mischief himself; but that, besides him, you had required and demanded two others who were in his Company when the Murders were committed. We promise faithfully, in our Return, to renew our Reproofs, and to charge the *Delawares* to send down some of their Chiefs with these two young Men (but not as Prisoners) to be examined by you; and as we think, upon Examination, you will not find them guilty, we rely on your Justice not to do them any Harm, but to permit them to return home in Safety.

WE likewise understand, that Search has been made for the Goods belonging to the Deceased, and that some have been already returned to your People, but that some are still missing. You may depend upon our giving the strictest Charge to the *Delawares* to search again with more Diligence for the Goods, and to return them, or the Value of them, in Skins. And, to confirm what we have said, we give you this String of Wampum.

Which was received with the usual Ceremonies.

Brother Onas,

The *Conoy Indians* have informed us, that they sent you a Message, some Time ago, to advise you, that they were ill used by the white People in the Place where they had lived, and that they had come to a Resolution of removing to *Shamokin*, and requested some small Satisfaction for their Land; and as they never have received any Answer from you, they have desired us to speak for them; we heartily recommend their Case to your Generosity. And, to give Weight to our Recommendation, we present you with this String of Wampum.

Which was received with the usual Ceremony.

The Governor having conferred a little Time with the honourable

Commissioners of Virginia *and* Maryland*, made the following Reply:*

Brethren,

I am glad to find that you agree with me in the Necessity of keeping the Road between us clear and open, and the Concern you have expressed on account of the barbarous Murders mentioned to you, is a Proof of your Brotherly Affection for us. If Crimes of this Nature be not strictly enquired into, and the Criminals severely punished, there will be an End of all Commerce between us and the *Indians*, and then you will be altogether in the Power of the *French*. They will set what Price they please on their own Goods, and give you what they think fit for your Skins; so it is for your own Interest that our Traders should be safe in their Persons and Goods when they travel to your Towns.

Brethren,

I considered this Matter well before I came from *Philadelphia*, and I advised with the Council there upon it, as I have done here with the honourable the Commissioners of *Virginia* and *Maryland*. I never heard before of the Murder of the three *Indians* at *Ohio*; had Complaint been made to me of it, and it had appeared to have been committed by any of the People under my Government, they should have been put to Death, as two of them were, some Years ago, for killing two *Indians*. You are not to take your own Satisfaction, but to apply to me, and I will see that Justice be done you; and should any of the *Indians* rob or murder any of our People, I do expect that you will deliver them up to be tried and punished in the same Manner as white People are. This is the Way to preserve Friendship between us, and will be for your Benefit as well as ours. I am well pleased with the Steps you have already taken, and the Reproofs you have given to your Cousins the *Delawares*, and do expect you will lay your Commands upon some of their Chiefs to bring down the two young Men that were present at the Murders; if they are not brought down, I shall look upon it as a Proof of their Guilt.

If, upon Examination, they shall be found not to have been concerned in the bloody Action, they shall be well used, and sent home in Safety: I will take it upon myself to see that they have no Injustice done them. An Inventory is taken of the Goods already restored, and I expect Satisfaction will be made for such as cannot be found, in Skins, according to their Promise.

I well remember the coming down of one of the *Conoy Indians* with a Paper, setting forth, That the *Conoys* had come to a Resolution to leave the Land reserved for them by the Proprietors, but he made no Complaint to me of ill Usage from the white People. The Reason he gave for their Removal was, That the settling of the white People all round them had made Deer scarce, and that therefore they chose to remove to *Juniata*[26] for the Benefit of Hunting. I ordered what they said to be entered in the Council-Book. The old Man's Expences were born, and a Blanket given him at his Return home. I have not yet heard from the Proprietors on this Head; but you may be assured, from the Favour and Justice they have always shewn to the *Indians*,

---

[26]*Juniata:* A tributary of the Susquehanna River.

that they will do every thing that can be reasonably expected of them in this Case.

In the COURT-HOUSE Chamber at *Lancaster, July* 2, 1744, *P. M.*

P R E S E N T ,

The Honourable the Commissioners of *Virginia.*
The Deputies of the *Six Nations.*
Conrad Weiser, Interpreter.

The Indians *being told, by the Interpreter, that their Brother* Assaragoa *was going to speak to them, the Commissioners spoke as follows:*
Sachims and Warriors, our Friends and Brethren,

"A s we have already said enough to you on the Subject of the Title to the Lands you claim from *Virginia,* we have no Occasion to say any thing more to you on that Head, but come directly to the Point.

WE have opened the Chest, and the Goods are now here before you; they cost Two Hundred Pounds *Pennsylvania* Money, and were bought by a Person recommended to us by the Governor of *Pennsylvania* with ready Cash. We ordered them to be good in their Kinds, and we believe they are so. These Goods, and Two Hundred Pounds in Gold, which lie on the Table, we will give you, our Brethren of the *Six Nations,* upon Condition that you immediately make a Deed recognizing the King's Right to all the Lands that are, or shall be, by his Majesty's Appointment in the Colony of *Virginia.*

As to the Road, we agree you shall have one, and the Regulation is in Paper, which the Interpreter now has in his Custody to shew you. The People of *Virginia* shall perform their Part, if you and your *Indians* perform theirs; we are your Brethren, and will do no Hardships to you, but, on the contrary, all the Kindness we can."

THE *Indians* agreed to what was said, and *Canassatego* desired they would represent their Case to the King, in order to have a further Consideration when the Settlement increased much further back. To which the Commissioners agreed, and promised they would make such a Representation faithfully and honestly; and, for their further Security that they would do so, they would give them a Writing, under their Hands and Seals, to that Purpose.

THEY desired that some Rum might be given them to drink on their Way home, which the Commissioners agreed to, and paid them in Gold for that Purpose, and the Carriage of their Goods from *Philadelphia*, Nine Pounds, Thirteen Shillings, and Three-pence, *Pennsylvania* Money.

Canassatego further said, That as their Brother *Tocarry-hogan* sent them Provision on the Road here, which kept them from starving, he hoped their Brother *Assaragoa* would do the same for them back, and have the Goods he gave them carried to the usual Place; which the Commissioners agreed to, and ordered Provisions and Carriages to be provided accordingly.

AFTER this Conference the Deed was produced, and the Interpreter explained it to them; and they, according to their Rank and Quality, put their Marks and Seals to it in the Presence of several Gentlemen of *Maryland*, *Pennsylvania* and *Virginia*; and when they delivered the Deed, *Canassatego* delivered it for the Use of their Father, the Great King, and hoped he would consider them; on which the Gentlemen and *Indians* then present gave three Shouts.

In the COURT-HOUSE at *Lancaster, Tuesday, July* 3, 1744, *A. M.*

PRESENT,

The Honourable *GEORGE THOMAS*, Esq; Governor, &c.
The Honourable the Commissioners of *Virginia*.
The Honourable the Commissioners of *Maryland*.
The Deputies of the *Six Nations*.
Conrad Weiser, Interpreter.

The GOVERNOR *spoke as follows:*

Friends and Brethren of the Six Nations,

A T a Treaty held with many of the Chiefs of your Nations Two Years ago, the Road between us was made clearer and wider; our Fire was enlarged, and our Friendship confirmed by an Exchange of Presents, and many other mutual good Offices.

WE think ourselves happy in having been instrumental to your meeting with our Brethren of *Virginia* and *Maryland*; and we persuade ourselves, that you, on your Parts, will always remember it as an Instance of our Good-will and Affection for you. This has given us an Opportunity of seeing you sooner than perhaps we should otherwise have done; and, as we are under mutual Obligations by Treaties, we to hear with our Ears for you, and you to hear with your Ears for us, we take this Opportunity to inform you of what very nearly concerns us both.

THE *Great King of* ENGLAND and the *French* King have declared War against each other. Two Battles have been fought, one by Land, and the other by Sea. The *Great King of* ENGLAND commanded the Land Army in Person, and gained a compleat Victory. Numbers of the *French* were killed and taken Prisoners, and the rest were forced to pass a River with Precipitation to save their Lives. The Great God covered the King's Head in that Battle, so that he did not receive the least Hurt; for which you, as well as we, have Reason to be very thankful.

THE Engagement at Sea was likewise to the Advantage of the *English*. The *French* and *Spaniards* joined their Ships together, and came out to fight us. The brave *English* Admiral burnt one of their largest Ships, and many others were so shattered, that they were glad to take the Opportunity of a very high Wind, and a dark Night, to run away, and to hide themselves again in their own Harbours. Had the Weather proved fair, he would, in all Probability, have taken or destroyed them all.

I need not put you in mind how much *William Penn* and his Sons have been your Friends, and the Friends of all the *Indians*. You have long and often experienced their Friendship for you; nor need I repeat to you how kindly you were treated, and what valuable Presents were made to you Two Years ago by the Governor, the Council, and the Assembly, of *Pennsylvania*. The Sons of *William Penn* are all now in *England*, and have left me in their Place, well knowing how much I regard you and all the *Indians*. As a fresh Proof of this, I have left my House, and am come thus far to see you, to renew our Treaties, to brighten the Covenant Chain, and to confirm our Friendship with you. In Testimony whereof, I present you with this Belt of Wampum.

Which was received with the Yo-hah.

As your Nations have engaged themselves by Treaty to assist us, your Brethren of *Pennsylvania*, in case of a War with the *French*, we do not doubt but you will punctually perform an Engagement so solemnly entred into. A War is now declared, and we expect that you will not suffer the *French*, or any of the *Indians* in Alliance with them, to march through your Country to disturb any of our Settlements; and that you will give us the earliest and best Intelligence of any Designs that may be formed by them to our Disadvantage, as we promise to do of any that may be to yours. To enforce what I have now said to you in the strongest Manner, I present you with this Belt of Wampum.

Which was received with the Yo-hah.

After a little Pause his Honour, the GOVERNOR, *spoke again:*
Friends and Brethren of the Six Nations,

WHAT I have now said to you is in Conformity to Treaties subsisting between the Province of which I am Governor and your Nations. I now proceed, with the Consent of the honourable Commissioners for *Virginia* and *Maryland,* to tell you, that all Differences having been adjusted, and the Roads between us and you made quite clear and open, we are ready to confirm our Treaties with your Nations, and establish a Friendship that is not to end, but with the World itself. And, in Behalf of the Province of *Pennsylvania,* I do, by this fine Belt of Wampum, and a Present of Goods, to the Value of Three Hundred Pounds, confirm and establish the said Treaties of Peace, Union and Friendship, you on your Parts doing the same.

Which was received with a loud Yo-hah.

THE Governor further added, The Goods bought with the One Hundred Pounds Sterling, put into my Hands by the Governor of *Virginia,* are ready to be delivered when you please. The Goods bought and sent up by the People of the Province of *Pennsylvania,* according to the List which the Interpreter will explain, are laid by themselves, and are likewise ready to be delivered to you at your own time.

After a little Pause the Commissioners of Virginia *spoke as follows:*
Sachems and Warriors of the Six Nations,

THE Way between us being made smooth by what passed Yesterday, we desire now to confirm all former Treaties made between *Virginia* and you, our Brethren of the *Six Nations,* and to make our Chain of Union and Friendship as bright as the Sun, that it may not contract any more Rust for ever; that our Childrens Children may rejoice at, and confirm what we have done; and that you and your Children may not forget it, we give you One Hundred Pounds in Gold, and this Belt of Wampum.

Which was received with the usual Ceremony.

Friends and Brethren,

ALTHO' we have been disappointed in our Endeavours to bring about a Peace between you and the *Catawbas,* yet we desire to speak to you something more about them. We believe they have been unfaithful to you, and spoke of you with a foolish Contempt; but this may be only the Rashness of some of their young Men. In this Time of War with our common Enemies the *French* and *Spaniards,* it will be the wisest Way to be at Peace among ourselves. They, the *Catawbas,* are also Children of the Great King, and therefore we desire you will agree, that we may endeavour to make a Peace between you and them, that we may be all united by one common Chain of Friendship. We give you this String of Wampum.

Which was received with the usual Ceremony.

Brethren,

OUR Friend, *Conrad Weiser,* when he is old, will go into the other World, as our Fathers have done; our Children will then want such a Friend to go between them and your Children, to reconcile any Differences that may happen to arise between them, that, like him, may have the Ears and Tongues of our Children and yours.

THE Way to have such a Friend, is for you to send three or four of your Boys to *Virginia,* where we have a fine House for them to live in, and a Man on purpose to teach the Children of you, our Friends, the Religion, Language and Customs of the white People. To this Place we kindly invite you to send some of your Children, and we promise you they shall have the same Care taken of them, and be instructed in the same Manner as our own Children, and be returned to you again when you please; and, to confirm this, we give you this String of Wampum.

Which was received with the usual Ceremony.

Then the Commissioners of Maryland *spoke as follows:*

Friends and Brethren, the Chiefs or Sachims of the Six *united* Nations,

THE Governor of *Maryland* invited you hither, we have treated you as Friends, and agreed with you as Brethren.

As the Treaty now made concerning the Lands in *Maryland* will, we hope, prevent effectually every future Misunderstanding between us on that Account, we will now bind faster the Links of our Chain of Friendship by a Renewal of all our former Treaties; and that they may still be the better secured, we shall present you with One Hundred Pounds in Gold.

WHAT we have further to say to you is, Let not our Chain contract any Rust; whenever you perceive the least Speck, tell us of it, and we will make it clean. This we also expect of you, that it may always continue so bright as our Generations may see their Faces in it; and, in Pledge of the Truth of what we have now spoken, and our Affection to you, we give you this Belt of Wampum.

Which was received with the usual Ceremony.

CANASSATEGO, in return, spoke as follows:

Brother Onas, Assaragoa, *and* Tocarry-hogan,

WE return you Thanks for your several Speeches, which are very agreeable to us. They contain Matters of such great Moment, that we propose to give them a very serious Consideration, and to answer them suitably to their Worth and Excellence; and this will take till To-morrow Morning, and when we are ready we will give you due Notice.

YOU tell us you beat the *French*; if so, you must have taken a great deal of Rum from them, and can the better spare us some of that Liquor to make us rejoice with you in the Victory.

THE Governor and Commissioners ordered a Dram[27] of Rum to be given to each in a small Glass, calling it, *A French Glass.*

In the COURT-HOUSE at *Lancaster, July* 4, 1744, *A. M.*

P R E S E N T ,

The Honourable *GEORGE THOMAS*, Esq; Governor, &c.
The Honourable the Commissioners of *Virginia.*
The Honourable the Commissioners of *Maryland.*
The Deputies of the *Six Nations.*
Conrad Weiser, Interpreter.

CANASSATEGO Speaker.

Brother Onas,

YESTERDAY you expressed your Satisfaction in having been instrumental to our meeting with our Brethren of *Virginia* and *Maryland*. We, in return, assure you, that we have great Pleasure in this Meeting, and thank you for the Part you have had in bringing us together, in order to create a good Understanding, and to clear the Road; and, in Token of our Gratitude, we present you with this String of Wampum.

Which was received with the usual Ceremony.

Brother Onas,

YOU was pleased Yesterday to inform us, "That War had been declared between the *Great King of* ENGLAND and the *French* King; that two great Battles had been fought, one by Land, and the other at Sea; with many other Particulars." We are glad to hear the Arms of the King of *England* were successful, and take part with you in your Joy

---

[27] *Dram:* A small amount.

on this Occasion. You then came nearer Home, and told us, "You had left your House, and were come thus far on Behalf of the whole People of *Pennsylvania* to see us; to renew your Treaties; to brighten the Covenant Chain, and to confirm your Friendship with us." We approve this Proposition; we thank you for it. We own, with Pleasure, that the Covenant Chain between us and *Pennsylvania* is of old Standing, and has never contracted any Rust; we wish it may always continue as bright as it has done hitherto; and, in Token of the Sincerity of our Wishes, we present you with this Belt of Wampum.

Which was received with the Yo-hah.

Brother Onas,

YOU was pleased Yesterday to remind us of our mutual Obligation to assist each other in case of a War with the *French*, and to repeat the Substance of what we ought to do by our Treaties with you; and that as a War had been already entered into with the *French*, you called upon us to assist you, and not to suffer the *French* to march through our Country to disturb any of your Settlements.

IN answer, We assure you we have all these Particulars in our Hearts; they are fresh in our Memory. We shall never forget that you and we have but one Heart, one Head, one Eye, one Ear, and one Hand. We shall have all your Country under our Eye, and take all the Care we can to prevent any Enemy from coming into it; and, in Proof of our Care, we must inform you, that before we came here, we told **Onantio*, our Father, as he is called, that neither he, nor any of his People, should come through our Country, to hurt our Brethren the *English*, or any of the Settlements belonging to them; there was Room enough at Sea to fight, there he might do what he pleased, but he should not come upon our Land to do any Damage to our Brethren. And you may depend upon our using our utmost Care to see this effectually done; and, in Token of our Sincerity, we present you with this Belt of Wampum.

Which was received with the usual Ceremony.

After some little Time the Interpreter said, Canassatego *had forgot something material, and desired to mend his Speech, and to do so as often as he should omit any thing of Moment, and thereupon he added:*

THE *Six Nations* have a great Authority and Influence over sundry Tribes of *Indians* in Alliance with the *French*, and particularly over the

---

*Onantio, the Governor of *Canada*. [Franklin note.]

praying *Indians*,[28] formerly a Part with ourselves, who stand in the very Gates of the *French*; and, to shew our further Care, we have engaged these very *Indians*, and other *Indian* Allies of the *French* for you. They will not join the *French* against you. They have agreed with us before we set out. We have put the Spirit of Antipathy against the *French* in those People. Our Interest is very considerable with them, and many other Nations, and as far as ever it extends, we shall use it for your Service.

THE Governor said, *Canassatego* did well to mend his Speech; he might always do it whenever his Memory should fail him in any Point of Consequence, and he thanked him for the very agreeable Addition.

Brother Assaragoa,

YOU told us Yesterday, that all Disputes with you being now at an End, you desired to confirm all former Treaties between *Virginia* and us, and to make our Chain of Union as bright as the Sun.

WE agree very heartily with you in these Propositions; we thank you for your good Inclinations; we desire you will pay no Regard to any idle Stories that may be told to our Prejudice. And, as the Dispute about the Land is now intirely over, and we perfectly reconciled, we hope, for the future, we shall not act towards each other but as becomes Brethren and hearty Friends.

WE are very willing to renew the Friendship with you, and to make it as firm as possible, for us and our Children with you and your Children to the latest Generation, and we desire you will imprint these Engagements on your Hearts in the strongest Manner; and, in Confirmation that we shall do the same, we give you this Belt of Wampum.

Which was received with Yo-hah *from the Interpreter and all the Nations.*

Brother Assaragoa,

YOU did let us know Yesterday, that tho' you had been disappointed in your Endeavours to bring about a Peace between us and the *Catawbas*, yet you would still do the best to bring such a Thing about. We are well pleased with your Design, and the more so, as we hear you know what sort of People the *Catawbas* are, that they are spiteful and offensive, and have treated us contemptuously. We are glad you know these Things of the *Catawbas*; we believe what you say to be true, that there are, notwithstanding, some amongst them who are wiser and

---

[28]*praying Indians*: Iroquois who had moved to Canada; many converted to Roman Catholicism.

better; and, as you say, they are your Brethren, and belong to the
Great King over the Water, we shall not be against a Peace on reasonable Terms, provided they will come to the Northward to treat about
it. In Confirmation of what we say, and to encourage you in your
Undertaking, we give you this String of Wampum.

Which was received with the usual Ceremonies.

Brother Assaragoa,

You told us likewise, you had a great House provided for the Education of Youth, and that there were several white People and *Indians*
Children there to learn Languages, and to write and read, and invited
us to send some of our Children amongst you, &c.

WE must let you know we love our Children too well to send them
so great a Way, and the *Indians* are not inclined to give their Children
Learning. We allow it to be good, and we thank you for your Invitation;
but our Customs differing from yours, you will be so good as to
excuse us.

WE hope **Tarachawagon* will be preserved by the good Spirit to a
good old Age; when he is gone under Ground, it will be then time
enough to look out for another; and no doubt but amongst so many
Thousands as there are in the World, one such Man may be found,
who will serve both Parties with the same Fidelity as *Tarachawagon*
does; while he lives there is no Room to complain. In Token of our
Thankfulness for your Invitation, we give you this String of Wampum.

Which was received with the usual Ceremony.

Brother Tocarry-hogan,

You told us Yesterday, that since there was now nothing in Controversy between us, and the Affair of the Land was settled to your Satisfaction, you would now brighten the Chain of Friendship which hath
subsisted between you and us ever since we became Brethren; we are
well pleased with the Proposition, and we thank you for it; we also are
inclined to renew all Treaties, and keep a good Correspondence with
you. You told us further, if ever we should perceive the Chain had contracted any Rust, to let you know, and you would take care to take the
Rust out, and preserve it bright. We agree with you in this, and shall,
on our Parts, do every thing to preserve a good Understanding, and
to live in the same Friendship with you as with our Brother *Onas*

---

*Tarachawagon, Conrad Weiser. [Franklin note.]

and *Assaragoa*; in Confirmation whereof, we give you this Belt of Wampum.

On which the usual Cry of Yo-hah *was given.*

Brethren,

WE have now finished our Answer to what you said to us Yesterday, and shall now proceed to *Indian* Affairs, that are not of so general a Concern.

Brother Assaragoa,

THERE lives a Nation of *Indians* on the other Side of your Country, the *Tuscaroraes*, who are our Friends, and with whom we hold Correspondence; but the Road between us and them has been stopped for some Time, on account of the Misbehaviour of some of our Warriors. We have opened a new Road for our Warriors, and they shall keep to that; but as that would be inconvenient for Messengers going to the *Tuscaroraes*, we desire they may go the old Road. We frequently send Messengers to one another, and shall have more Occasion to do so now that we have concluded a Peace with the *Cherikees*. To enforce our Request, we give you this String of Wampum.

Which was received with the usual Cry of Approbation.

Brother Assaragoa,

AMONG these *Tuscaroraes* there live a few Families of the *Conoy Indians*, who are desirous to leave them, and to remove to the rest of their Nation among us, and the straight Road from them to us lies through the Middle of your Country. We desire you will give them free Passage through *Virginia*, and furnish them with Passes; and, to enforce our Request, we give you this String of Wampum.

Which was received with the usual Cry of Approbation.

Brother Onas, Assaragoa, *and* Tocarry-hogan,

AT the Close of your respective Speeches Yesterday, you made us very handsome Presents, and we should return you something suitable to your Generosity; but, alas, we are poor, and shall ever remain so, as long as there are so many *Indian* Traders among us. Theirs and the white Peoples Cattle have eat up all the Grass, and made Deer scarce. However, we have provided a small Present for you, and tho' some of you gave us more than others, yet, as you are all equally our Brethren, we shall leave it to you to divide it as you please. —And then presented three Bundles of Skins, which were received with the usual Ceremony from the three Governments.

WE have one Thing further to say, and that is, We heartily recommend Union and a good Agreement between you our Brethren. Never disagree, but preserve a strict Friendship for one another, and thereby you, as well as we, will become the stronger.

OUR wise Forefathers established Union and Amity between the *Five Nations*; this has made us formidable; this has given us great Weight and Authority with our neighbouring Nations.

WE are a powerful Confederacy; and, by your observing the same Methods our wise Forefathers have taken, you will acquire fresh Strength and Power; therefore whatever befals you, never fall out one with another.

THE Governor replied:

THE honourable Commissioners of *Virginia* and *Maryland* have desired me to speak for them; therefore I, in Behalf of those Governments, as well as of the Province of *Pennsylvania*, return you Thanks for the many Proofs you have given in your Speeches of your Zeal for the Service of your Brethren the *English*, and in particular for your having so early engaged in a Neutrality the several tribes of *Indians* in the *French* Alliance. We do not doubt but you will faithfully discharge your Promises. As to your Presents, we never estimate these Things by their real Worth, but by the Disposition of the Giver. In this Light we accept them with great Pleasure, and put a high Value upon them. We are obliged to you for recommending Peace and good Agreement amongst ourselves. We are all Subjects, as well as you, of the Great King beyond the Water; and, in Duty to his Majesty, and from the good Affection we bear to each other, as well as from a Regard to our own Interest, we shall always be inclined to live in Friendship.

THEN the Commissioners of *Virginia* presented the Hundred Pounds in Gold, together with a Paper, containing a Promise to recommend the *Six Nations* for further Favour to the King; which they received with *Yo-hah*, and the Paper was given by them to *Conrad Weiser* to keep for them. The Commissioners likewise promised that their publick Messengers should not be molested in their Passage through *Virginia*, and that they would prepare Passes for such of the *Conoy Indians* as were willing to remove to the Northward.

THEN the Commissioners of *Maryland* presented their Hundred Pounds in Gold, which was likewise received with the *Yo-hah*.

Canassatego said, We mentioned to you Yesterday the Booty you had taken from the *French*, and asked you for some of the Rum which we supposed to be Part of it, and you gave us some; but it turned out unfortunately that you gave us it in *French* Glasses, we now desire you will give us some in *English* Glasses.

THE Governor made answer, We are glad to hear you have such a Dislike for what is *French*. They cheat you in your Glasses, as well as in every thing else. You must consider we are at a Distance from *Williamsburg, Annapolis*, and *Philadelphia*, where our Rum Stores are, and that altho' we brought up a good Quantity with us, you have almost drunk it out; but, notwithstanding this, we have enough left to fill our *English* Glasses, and will shew the Difference between the Narrowness of the *French*, and the Generosity of your Brethren the *English* towards you.

THE *Indians* gave, in their Order, five *Yo-hahs*; and the honourable Governor and Commissioners calling for some Rum, and some middle sized Wine Glasses, drank Health to the *Great King of* ENGLAND and the *Six Nations*, and put an End to the Treaty by three loud Huzza's, in which all the Company joined.

IN the Evening the Governor went to take his Leave of the *Indians*, and, presenting them with a String of Wampum, he told them, that was in return for one he had received of them, with a Message to desire the Governor of *Virginia* to suffer their Warriors to go through *Virginia* unmolested, which was rendered unnecessary by the present Treaty.

THEN, presenting them with another String of Wampum, he told them, that was in return for theirs, praying him, that as they had taken away one Part of *Conrad Weiser*'s Beard,[29] which frightened their Children, he would please to take away the other, which he had ordered to be done.

The Indians *received these two Strings of Wampum with the usual* Yo-hah.

THE Governor then asked them, what was the Reason that more of the *Shawanaes*, from their Town on *Hohio*, were not at the Treaty? But seeing that it would require a Council in Form, and perhaps another Day to give an Answer, he desired they would give an Answer to *Conrad Weiser* upon the Road on their Return home, for he was to set out for *Philadelphia* the next Morning.

CANASSATEGO in Conclusion spoke as follows:

---

[29] *Conrad Weiser's Beard*: For a time during the 1730s and early 1740s Weiser had joined the mystical sect gathered at Ephrata Cloisters near Lancaster; one symbol of his attachment was growing a long beard, just as a sign of Weiser's disillusionment was his trimming that beard, probably after his return from Onondaga in August 1743. The Iroquois, teasing him, wanted it gone completely. See Paul A. W. Wallace, *Conrad Weiser, 1696–1760: Friend of Colonist and Mohawk* (Philadelphia: University of Pennsylvania Press, 1945), 105, 159, 174, 194.

WE have been hindered, by a great deal of Business, from waiting on you, to have some private Conversation with you, chiefly to enquire after the Healths of *Onas* beyond the Water; we desire you will tell them, we have a grateful Sense of all their Kindnesses for the *Indians*. Brother *Onas* told us, when he went away, he would not stay long from us; we think it is a great While, and want to know when we may expect him, and desire, when you write, you will recommend us heartily to him; which the Governor promised to do, and then took his Leave of them.

THE Commissioners of *Virginia* gave *Canassatego* a Scarlet Camblet[30] Coat, and took their Leave of them in Form, and at the same time delivered the Passes to them, according to their Request.

THE Commissioners of *Maryland* presented *Gachradodow* with a broad Gold-laced Hat, and took their Leave of them in the same Manner.

A true Copy, compared by   *RICHARD PETERS*, Secry.

T H E   E N D.

---

[30] *Camblet* (camlet): "Beautiful and costly eastern fabric," allegedly made first from camel's hair and silk, and later from wool and silk (*Oxford English Dictionary*).

PART THREE

Related Documents

1

BENJAMIN WEST

The Indians Giving a Talk to Colonel Bouquet . . . in Oct. 1764

1766

This engraving—based on a picture by Benjamin West (1738–1820), a Pennsylvania-born artist who became a renowned painter in London— offers a rare glimpse of a treaty council in the colonial era. It depicts a conference held near the Muskingum River in modern-day Ohio be- tween British Colonel Henry Bouquet and delegates from the Delawares, Shawnees, and Senecas living in the area. A major frontier war—often called Pontiac's Rebellion after an Ottawa war leader—had been raging for more than a year when Bouquet marched into Indian country at the head of an army, ready for battle but eager to talk peace with Britain's native foes. Though this "Conference at a Council Fire" was held twenty years after the 1744 Lancaster Treaty and several hundred miles farther

[William Smith], *An Historical Account of the Expedition against the Ohio Indians, in the year MDCCLXIV, under the Command of Henry Bouquet, Esq.* . . . (London, 1766). Image courtesy of the Rosenbach Museum and Library, Philadelphia.

west, it nonetheless captures some of the key ingredients of the talks in Lancaster between the Iroquois and the colonists. How does this scene compare with the written descriptions elsewhere in this volume of a treaty council's proceedings and participants? How can you explain the similarities and differences you find?

2

JOHN BARTRAM

Observations on a Visit to Onondaga

July–August 1743

John Bartram (1699–1777) was a Pennsylvania naturalist who traveled throughout the colonies collecting specimens of American plants and animals to send to scientists in Europe. In the summer of 1743 he and the cartographer Lewis Evans (c. 1700–1756) tagged along with the go-betweens Conrad Weiser and Shickellamy (see Major Figures in the Lancaster Treaty of 1744) on a diplomatic mission to the Iroquois capital at Onondaga. The journey had two goals: first, to begin repairing the damage done the previous winter by a skirmish between an Iroquois war party and Virginia frontiersmen; second, to pave the way for the formal treaty between Iroquois and colonial leaders that ultimately would take place at Lancaster the following year. Bartram, a tourist visiting Iroquois Country for the first time, found everything literally remarkable— that is, worthy of remark. As a result, he penned vivid descriptions both of everyday features of Iroquois life (food, houses, games) at this important moment in their history and of the rich ceremonial trappings of their formal councils. Compare Bartram's account with the report by Weiser, the veteran Iroquois expert (Document 3). How are the two similar or different, and what accounts for this?

Bartram set out from his farm near Philadelphia with Evans on July 3, 1743, heading for Conrad Weiser's home at Tulpehocken, some seventy miles northwest of the provincial capital. From there they made for Shamokin, a major Indian town at the junction of the Susquehanna River's two branches, where Shickellamy lived. On July 10, the party left Shamokin, bound for Onondaga. Eleven days later, they arrived at their destination.

. . . We descended easily for several miles, over good land producing sugar-maples, many of which the *Indians* had tapped to make sugar of

---

John Bartram, *Observations on the Inhabitants, Climate, Soil, Rivers, Productions, Animals, and other matters worthy of Notice. Made by John Bartram, In his Travels from Pensilvania to Onondago, Oswego and the Lake Ontario, In Canada*. . . (London: J. Whiston and B. White, 1751), 39–44, 58–61.

the sap, also oaks, hickery, white walnuts, plums and some apple trees, full of fruit; the *Indians* had set long bushes all round the trees at a little distance, I suppose to keep the small children from stealing the fruit before they were ripe: here we halted and turned our horses to grass, while the inhabitants cleared a cabin for our reception; they brought us victuals, and we dispatched a messenger immediately to *Onondago* to let them know how near we were, it being within 4 miles. All the *Indians*, men, women, and children came to gaze at us and our horses, the little boys and girls climbed on the roofs of their cabins, about ten in number to enjoy a fuller view, we set out about ten, and travelled over good land all the way, mostly an easy descent, some lime-stone, then down the east hill, over ridges of lime-stone rock, but generally a moderate descent into the fine vale where this capital (if I may so call it) is situated.

We alighted at the council house, where the chiefs were already assembled to receive us, which they did with a grave chearful complaisance, according to their custom; they shew'd us where to lay our baggage, and repose ourselves during our stay with them; which was in the two end apartments of this large house. The *Indians* that came with us, were placed over against us: this cabin is about 80 feet long, and 17 broad, the common passage 6 feet wide, and the apartments on each side 5 feet, raised a foot above the passage by a long sapling hewed square, and fitted with joists that go from it to the back of the house; on these joists they lay large pieces of bark, and on extraordinary occasions spread matts made of rushes, this favour we had; on these floors they set or lye down every one as he will, the apartments are divided from each other by boards or bark, 6 or 7 foot long, from the lower floor to the upper, on which they put their lumber,[1] when they have eaten their homony,[2] as they set in each apartment before the fire, they can put the bowel over head, having not above 5 foot to reach; they set on the floor sometimes at each end, but mostly at one: they have a shed to put their wood into in the winter, or in the summer, to set to converse or play, that has a door to the south; all the sides and roof of the cabin is made of bark, bound fast to poles set in the ground, and bent round on the top, or set aflatt, for the roof as we set our rafters; over each fire place they leave a hole to let out the

---

[1] *lumber*: "Disused articles of furniture and the like, which take up room inconveniently, or are removed to be out of the way; useless odds and ends" (*Oxford English Dictionary*).

[2] *homony* (hominy): Coarsely ground corn boiled with water.

smoak, which in rainy weather, they cover with a piece of bark, and this they can easily reach with a pole to push it on one side or quite over the hole, after this model are most of their cabins built. . . .

The fine vale of *Onondago* runs north and south, a little inclining to the west, and is near a mile wide, where the town is situated and excellent soil, the river that divides this charming vale, is 2, 3 or 4 foot deep, very full of trees fallen across, or drove on heaps by the torrents. The town in its present state is about 2 or 3 miles long, yet the scattered cabins on both sides the water, are not above 40 in number, many of them hold 2 families, but all stand single, and rarely above 4 or 5 near one another; so that the whole town is a strange mixture of cabins, interspersed with great patches of high grass, bushes and shrubs, some of pease, corn and squashes, lime-stone bottom composed of fossils and sea shells. . . .

At night, soon after we were laid down to sleep, and our fire almost burnt out, we were entertained by a comical fellow, disguised in as odd a dress as *Indian* folly could invent; he had on a clumsy vizard of wood colour'd black, with a nose 4 or 5 inches long, a grining mouth set awry, furnished with long teeth, round the eyes circles of bright brass, surrounded by a larger circle of white paint, from his forehead hung long tresses of buffaloes hair, and from the catch part of his head ropes made of the plated[3] husks of *Indian* corn; I cannot recollect the whole of his dress, but that it was equally uncouth: he carried in one hand a large staff, in the other a calabash[4] with small stones in it, for a rattle, and this he rubbed up and down his staff; he would sometimes hold up his head and make a hideous noise like the braying of an ass; he came in at the further end, and made this noise at first, whether it was because he would not surprise us too suddenly I can't say: I ask'd *Conrad Weiser*, who as well as myself lay next the alley, what noise that was? and *Shickalamy* the *Indian* chief, our companion, who I supposed, thought me somewhat scared, called out, lye still *John*, I never heard him speak so much plain *English* before. The jack-pudding[5] presently came up to us, and an *Indian* boy came with him and kindled our fire, that we might see his glittering eyes and antick postures as he hobbled round the fire, sometimes he would turn the Buffaloes hair on one side that we might take the better view

---

[3] *plated*: Probably pleated.
[4] *calabash*: A hollowed-out gourd or pumpkin.
[5] *jack-pudding*: A buffoon or clown.

of his ill-favoured phyz,[6] when he had tired himself, which was some-time after he had well tired us, the boy that attended him struck 2 or 3 smart blows on the floor, at which the hobgoblin seemed surprised and on repeating them he jumped fairly out of doors and disappeared. I suppose this was to divert us and get some tobacco for himself, for as he danced about he would hold out his hand to any he came by to receive this gratification which as often as any one gave him he would return an awkward compliment. By this I found it no new diversion to any but my self. . . .[7] After this farce we endeavoured to compose our-selves to sleep but towards morning was again disturbed by a drunken *Squaw* coming into the cabin frequently complimenting us and singing. . . .

[While Weiser and Shickellamy remained in town to hold preliminary talks with Iroquois leaders (see Document 3), Bartram and Evans hired an Indian guide to take them on a side trip to Lake Ontario. They returned on the evening of July 27 to find "deputies" from various Iroquois nations still assembling for the council. By July 30, the proceedings were ready to begin.]

This afternoon the chiefs met in council, and three of them spoke for near a quarter of an hour each, two of these while speaking, walked backward and forward in the common passage, near 2 thirds of its length, with a slow even pace, and much composure and gravity in their countenance; the other delivered what he had to say sitting in the middle, in a graceful tone exhorting them to a close indissoluble amity and unanimity, for it was by this perfect union their forefath-ers had conquered their enemies, were respected by their allies, and honoured by all the world; that they were now met according to their antient custom, tho' several imminent dangers stood in their way, mountains, rivers, snakes and evil spirits, but that by the assistance of the *great Spirit* they now saw each others faces according to ap-pointment.

This the interpreter told me was the opening of the diet,[8] and was in the opinion of these people abundantly sufficient for one day, since

---

[6]*phyz*, or *phiz*: Face.

[7]*The jack-pudding . . . myself. . . .*: The party had been visited by a member of the Iro-quois Society of Faces (*gagosa*, "face"), a medicine society that cured ailments, banished evil spirits, and otherwise patrolled the boundaries of proper behavior. It is unclear whether this was entertainment, as Bartram thought, or an effort to drive out any evils the strangers might have brought into the village. See William N. Fenton, *False Faces of the Iroquois* (Norman: University of Oklahoma Press, 1987).

[8]*diet*: Legislature or assembly.

there is nothing they contemn so much as precipitation in publick councils; indeed they esteem it at all times a mark of much levity in any one to return an immediate answer to a serious question however obvious, and they consequently spin out a Treaty, where many points are to be moved, to a great length of time, as is evident from what our conference with them, produced afterward at *Lancaster* begun the 22d of *June* 1744.

This council was followed by a feast, after 4 o'clock we all dined together upon 4 great kettles of *Indian* corn soop, which we soon emptied, and then every chief retired to his home.

31*st*, In the morning, as soon as light, I walked out to look at our horses as usual, and close by a cabin spied a knife almost covered with grass; I supposed it lost, but the *Indians* being not yet stiring let it lie: a little after sun-rise I walked there again, and the *Squaw* being at the door, shewed her where it lay, at which she seemed exceeding pleased, and picked it up immediately. As I came back to our cabin, I spy'd 2 *Indian* girls at play with beans, which they threw from one to the other on a match coat[9] spread between them;[10] as they were behind our cabin, I turned to see how they play'd, but they seemed much out of countenance,[11] and run off in an instant: I observed that the *Indian* women are generally very modest.

About noon the council sat a 2*d* time, and our interpreter had his audience, being charge by the governor with the conduct of the treaty. *Conrad Weiser* had engaged the *Indian* speaker to open the affair to the chiefs assembled in council; he made a speech near half an hour, and delived [*sic*] 3 broad belts and 5 strings of *Wampum* to the council, on the proper occasions. There was a pole laid a-cross from one chamber to another over the passage, on this their belts and strings were hung, that all the council might see them, and here have the matters in remembrance, in confirmation of which they were delivered: The conference held till 3, after which we dined, this repast consisted of 3 great kettles of *Indian* corn soop, or thin homony, with dry'd eels and other fish boiled in it, and one kettle full of young squashes and their flowers boiled in water, and a little meal mixed; this dish was but weak food, last of all was served a great bowl, full of

---

[9]*match coat*: A loose-fitting coat or cloak commonly worn by Native Americans in eastern North America, usually made of coarse wool or cloth.

[10]*As I came back . . . between them*: Perhaps a variation of *Gus-ga-e-sá-ta*, or "Deer-buttons." See Lewis H. Morgan, *League of the Ho-Dé-No-Sau-Nee or Iroquois* (New York: Dodd, Mead, 1922), I, 290–91.

[11]*out of countenance*: Annoyed, out of sorts.

Indian dumplings, made of new sost[12] corn, cut or scraped off the ear, then with the addition of some boiled beans, lapped[13] well up in *Indian* corn leaves, this is good hearty provision. After dinner, we had a favourable answer, coroborated by several belts of *Wampum*, with a short speech to each, these we carried away as our tokens of peace and friendship, the harangue concluded with a charge to sit still as yet, for tho' they had dispatched our business first, it was not because they were weary of us, but to make us easy.[14] This complement preceded other business, which lasted till near sun set, when we regaled on a great bowl of boiled cakes, 6 or 7 inches diameter, and about 2 thick, with another of boiled squash; soon after, the chiefs in a friendly manner took their leave of us, and departed every one to his lodging: this night we treated two of the chiefs that lived in the council hall, which as I mentioned, was our quarters; they drank chearfully, wishing a long continuance of uninterrupted amity between the *Indians* and *English*.

[12] *sost* (sossed?): "A sloppy mess or mixture; a dish of food having this character" (*Oxford English Dictionary*).
[13] *lapped*: "Wrapped" (*Oxford English Dictionary*).
[14] *make us easy*: Put us at ease, relaxed.

3

CONRAD WEISER

Report on the Council Proceedings at Onondaga

July–August 1743

By 1743 Weiser was already an experienced and respected go-between, but rarely were his skills needed more than that year, after a skirmish between Iroquois warriors and Virginia frontiersmen pushed the region toward the brink of war. To avert that conflict, Weiser worked with

Minutes of the Provincial Council of Pennsylvania, From the Organization to the Termination of the Proprietary Government, Vol. IV (Harrisburg, Pa.: Theo. Fenn & Co., 1851), 660–69. Editor's note: I have kept Weiser's original (and often eccentric) spelling, except to change the lowercase "double f" to a capital "F" (thus, *ffriendship* becomes *Friendship*). I have also added some paragraph breaks and made quotation marks consistent for the sake of clarity.

native and colonial leaders, getting Virginia to send kind words and a lavish gift to Onondaga. Bearing that good news, in July he left his Pennsylvania home, accompanied by the naturalist John Bartram (see Document 2) and the cartographer Lewis Evans, and headed north, picking up the Oneida leader Shickellamy en route. Weiser's description of the talks at Onondaga has been called the best surviving account of Iroquois diplomatic protocol. How does an official report penned by a veteran like Weiser compare with the journal of the same visit to Onondaga kept by Bartram, a newcomer? How did the talks at Onondaga in 1743 compare with their counterpart at Lancaster the following summer?

Conrad Weiser's Report of his Journey to Onondago on the affairs of Virginia, in Obedience to the Orders of the Governor in Council, 13 June, 1743, delivered to the Governor the 1st September:

On the 21st [July] we arrived at Cachiadachse, the first Town of the Onondagoes. About noon I heard that the Messenger I had sent from Oswego had missed his Way and did not arrive there. I therefore imediately sent a Messenger from this place to the Chief Town about five miles off to acquaint the Chiefs of that Nation of my coming with a Message from Onas on behalf of Assaryquoa.[1] They dispatched Messengers that Day to Summon the Council of the Six Nations. My Messenger came back & inform'd me that the House of Annwaraogon was appointed for our Lodging; we set out and arriv'd there at three o'Clock in the Afternoon. After we had eat some dry'd Eels boiled in Hominy,[2] and some Matts had been spread for Us to lye upon, Canassatego & Caheshcarowanoto,[3] of the Chiefs, with several more, came to see Us & receiv'd Us very kindly. They asked how their Brethren did in Philadelphia, and in particular the Governor, & whether Onas[4] was arrived. I answer'd that their Brethren in Philadelphia were all well & in the same Disposition of Mind as they had left them in Last Year, and in particular the Governor their Brother was so, who, according to the Trust reposed in him by Onas, when he left Philadelphia, was always engaged for the good of the Publick. We smoak'd a

---

[1] *Assaryquoa*: For this and other Iroquois names for different colonies, see "Major Figures in the Lancaster Treaty of 1744."

[2] *Hominy*: coarsely ground corn boiled with water.

[3] *Caheshcarowanoto* (Caheshcarowno, Kaheskarowaneh[?]): "The head chief at the time." William N. Fenton, *The Great Law and the Longhouse: A Political History of the Iroquois Confederacy* (Norman: University of Oklahoma Press, 1998), 418.

[4] *Onas*: The proprietors of Pennsylvania: Thomas, Richard, or John Penn, sons of William Penn, the founder of the province.

Pipe of Philadelphia Tobacco together, & had some further discourse on things of no Consequence.

The 22d, early in the Morning, Tocanontie (otherwise call'd the black Prince of Onondago), came to see Us with Caxhayion[5] and expressed their Satisfaction at my coming to Onondago, saying You never come without good News from our Brethren in Philadelphia. I smil'd & told him it was enough to kill a Man to come such a Long & bad Road over Hills, Rocks, Old Trees, and Rivers, and to fight through a Cloud of Vermine, and all kinds of Poisen'd Worms and creeping things, besides being Loaded with a disagreeable Message, upon which they laugh'd; and Tocanontie told me that he was extreamely glad last Night to hear I was come to Onondago. Canassatego and Caheshcarowno, with several more, came to see Us again and spent the Day with us. We had for the Subject of our Conversation the Occurrences of our Journey and General News.

The twenty-third it was good weather. I, with Shikellimo, visited Canassatego, desired him to meet Us in the Bushes to have a private Discourse, which he approved of. We met a little way distant from the Town; I brought with me my Instructions and the Wampums I had, and told him that as he was our Particular Friend and well acquainted both with Indians & white People's Affairs & Customs, I would tell him all my Business, and beg his Advice how to speak to everything when the Council should be met. He assured me of his good will and Affection to the Governor of Pensilvania and all his People, and that he would do for me what lay in his power. I then explained my Instructions to him, and show'd him the Wampum. He told us that what he had heard of [from] me was very good, he must first go and acquaint Caheshcarowano with it, and they would then both send for me and Shikellimo, and put us in the Way; we broke up imediately, and Canassatego went directly to Caheshcarowano and we to our Lodging.

In the afternoon they sent for me and Shikellimo to the House of Caheshcarowano, and I was desired to bring my Instructions and my Wampums with me. I went along with the Messenger to the House of the said Chief, where I found, to my Surprize, all the Chiefs of Onondago met in Council. Tocanontie spoke to me after this Manner: "Brother, the Chiefs of Onondago are all of one Body and Soul,

---

[5] *Caxhaiyon* (Coxhayion) (?–1749): An Onondaga headman who had been at treaties with Pennsylvania in 1736 and 1742. He died during another journey to that province for talks in 1749. Francis Jennings et al., eds., *Iroquois Indians: A Documentary History of the Diplomacy of the Six Nations and Their League: Guide to the Microfilm Collection* (Woodbridge, Conn.: Research Publications, 1985), 462.

and of one Mind; therefore Canassatego and Cahescarowano have acquainted us with the whole of what had passed betwixt You and Canassatego in the Bushes; you have done very well and prudent to inform the Onondagoes of your Message before the rest of the Coun- sellors meet, since it Concerns chiefly the Onondagoes, and it will altogether be left to Us by the Council of the United Nations to answer your Message; be, therefore, not surprized in seeing Us all Met in Council unexpectedly, and explain the Paper to Us you have from our Brother the Governor of Pennsylvania," which I did accordingly, and acquainted them with the whole Message; they seemed to be very well pleased, and promised they would put every thing in such Pos- ture that when the Council of the United Nations arrive, I should have an Answer soon, and such an one as they did not doubt would be satis- factory to the Governor of Pennsylvania and Assaryquoa; that they had always so much regard for Onas & his People that they would do any- thing for them in their Power, and they looked upon the Person that kept House for Onas (meaning the Governor) as if Onas was there himself. I thanked them for their good will and Left them for this Time, knowing they had something to do amongst themselves; Tocanontie was Speaker.

The 24th the Council of the Onandagoes sat again. Jonnhaty, the Captain of the Unhappy Company that had the Skirmish last winter in Virginia, was sent for with two More of his Companions. He was desired to tell the story from the beginning how every thing happen'd, which he did; he seem'd to be a very thoughtful and honest Man, and took a deal of Time in telling the Story; after he had done, I told him I would write it down before I left Onondago, in his Presence, to which he agreed, and desired that some of the Chiefs might be present when he was to rehearse it again. In the Evening the Cajuga Deputies arrived.

The 25th Visited Caheshcarowano this Morning, and Caxhayion in the afternoon. Jonnhaty gave a Feast to which Assaryquoa whom I represented, and Onas whom Shikellimo represented, was invited with the Chiefs of the Town, about 18 in number; the Feast consisted of a Cask of Rum, of about two gallons; several Songs were sung before the Feast begun, in which they thanked Assaryquo for visiting them; they also thanked Onas (the Governor of Pennsilvania) for conduct- ing Assaryquoa and Showing him the Way to Onondago; the Sun was praised for having given Light, and for dispelling the Clouds; then the Cask was open'd, & a Cup of about ¾ of a Gill[6] was fill'd for

---

[6]*Gill*: Approximately one quarter of a pint.

Canassatego, who drank to the Health of Assaryquoa; next him drank Caheshcarowano to the Health of the Governor of Pennsilvania, and after this Manner we drank round; the next Time the first Cup was reached to me by Jonnhaty, who attended the Feast, I wished long Life to the wise Counsellors of the united Nations, and drank my Cup, so did Shikellimo & the rest; after that the Kettle was handed round with a wooden Spoon in it; every one took so much as he pleased. Whilst we were drinking & smoking, news came that a Deputation of the Nanticoke Indians arrived at Cachiadachse from Maryland; the House of Canassatego was ordain'd for them, since the Town House was taken up by Onas & Assaryquoa; after all the Rum was drunk, the usual thanks was given from every Nation or Deputy with the usual sound of Jo-haa, and we parted.

The 26th. In the Morning I went to see the Nantikokes; there was six in Number, none could speak a word of the Language of the united Nations. I found there besides Canassetego, his Brother, Zila Woolien, and others; they desired me to stand Interpreter for the Nanticokes (they heard us talk English together), to which I consented; no Deputies were Yet arrived from any other Nation. I desired Canassatego to send again to have at least the Oneidos there, as they were concern'd in the Late Skirmish, which was done immediately.

The 27th. No Business was done to-Day.

The 28th. The Deputies from the Oneidos and Tuscaroros arriv'd. Aquoyiota, an old Acquaintance of mine, came with them; he is a Man of about 70 Years of age, a Native & Chief of the Oneidos.

The 29th. The Onondago's held another Private Council, and sent for me and Shikellimo; every thing was discoursed over again, and we agreed that Canassatego should speak in behalf of the Government of Virginia; and the Wampums were divided into so many parts as there were Articles to be spoken of; and the Goods were to be divided between the family's in Mourning and the Publick Council of the united Nations. A Messenger was sent to hasten the Mohawks away from the Oneider Lake, where it was supposed they tarried; they arrived, five in Number.

The 30th, About noon, the Council then met at our Lodging and declared themselves compleat, and a deal of Ceremonies Passed; First the Onondagoes rehearsed the beginning of the Union of the five Nations, Praised their Grandfathers' Wisdom in establishing the Union or Alliance, by which they became a formidable Body; that they (now living) were but Fools to their wise Fathers, Yet protected and accompanied by their Fathers' Spirit; and then the discourse was directed to the Deputies of the several Nations, and to the Messengers from Onas and Assaryquoa, then to the Nanticokes, to welcome them all to the Council Fire which was now kindled. A String of Wampum was given by Tocanontie, in behalf of the Onondagoes, to wipe off the Sweat from their (the Deputies & Messenger's) Bodies, and God, who had protected them all against the Evil Spirits in the Woods, who were always doing mischief to people travelling to Onondago, was praised. All this was done by way of a Song, the Speaker walking up & down in the House.

After this the Deputies & Messengers held a Conference by themselves, and appointed Aquoyiota to return thanks for their kind reception, with another String of Wampum. Aquoyiota repeated all that was said in a Singing way, walking up and down in the House, added more in Praise of their wise Fathers and of the happy union, repeated all the Names of those Ancient Chiefs that establish'd it; they no Doubt, said he, are now God's and dwell in heaven; then Proclamation was made that the Council was now Opened, and Assaryquoa was to speak next morning in the same House, and due Attendance should be given. All those Indian Ceremonies took up that afternoon. Jo-haas from every Nation was given.

The 31st, about Ten of the Clock, the Council of the united Nations met, and Zila Woolien gave me Notice that they were now ready to hear Onas and Assaryquoa Speak. I called Canassatego and desired him to speak for me in Open Council, as I would tell him, Article by Article (according to what was first agreed upon), which he Proclaim'd to the Council, and they approv'd of it, because they knew it required some Ceremonies with which I was not acquainted.

The Speaker then begun and made the following Narrative: "*Brethren the United Nations*, you Togarg Hogon our Brother, Nittaruntaquaa our Son, also Sonnawantowano and Tuscaroro, our Younger Sons, you, also, our absent Brother Ounghcarrydawy dionen Horarrawe,[7] Know Ye, that what was transacted last Winter at this Fire by Us and our Brother Onas, on behalf of our Brother the Governor of Virginia, known to Us by the Name of Assaryquoa, was all carefully put down in Writing and sent to Assaryquoa, our Brother, by our Brother Onas, upon the Receipt whereof our Brother Assaryquoa

---

[7] *Togarg Hogon*: Tekarihoken, Mohawks. *Nittaruntaquaa*: Nitarontakowa, "they of the great log," Oneidas. *Sonnawantowano*: Sononnawentona, "great pipe people," Cayugas. *Tuscaroro*: Tuscaroras. *Ounghcarrydawy dionen Horarrawe*: Probably Senecas. Fenton, *Great Law*, 419.

wrote again to our Brother Onas and thank'd him kindly for his Mediation in healing the Breach occasion'd by the Late unhappy Skirmish, and requested the Continuance of our Brother Onas' good Offices; and that the Interpreter might be sent to Sagogsaanagechtheyky[8] with such Instructions as Onas our Brother (who knowing the Nature, Customs, and the very Heart of his Brethren) shall think fit. This is all what I have to say about what is past. Now you will hear our Brother Assaryquoa himself, who has been brought to our Fire by our Brother Onas."

Then I took up a Belt of Wampum and told the Speaker, Canassatego, a few Words, and he proceeded and Spoke in behalf of the Governor of Virginia as follows:

"S.—Brethren, The United Nations now met in Council at Sagoghsaanagechtheyky; when I heard of the late unhappy Skirmish that happened in my Country between some of your Warriours and my People, I was Surprized. I could not account for it to my self why such a thing should happen between Brethren. This Belt of Wampum, therefore, I give to the Familys in Mourning amongst You my Brethren at Sagoghsaanagechchayky, to condole with them and moderate their Grief."

The Belt was given and the usual Sound of Approbation was returned by the whole House;

—2. Then I handed another Belt to the Speaker and Spoke to him; he spoke much the same as before, and desired that Belt might be given to the Familys in Mourning at Niharuntaquoa, or the Oneidos, for the same Use. Thanks was given again by the whole Assembly with the usual Sound, then I handed a large Belt to the Speaker.

—3. "Brethren of the united Nations, the Sun kept back his beams from Us, and a dark Cloud overshadow'd us when the Late unhappy Skirmish happened between my People and Your Warriors. My People are charged with having begun Hostilities; I will not Dispute with you about it. It is most certain that an Evil Spirit which governs in Darkness has been the Promoter of it, for Brethren will never fall out without giving Ear to such Evil Spirits. I and the Old and wise People of my Country highly Disapproved the Action, I therefore came here to your fire to fetch home the Hatchet, from an Apprehension that it might have been unadvisedly made Use of by my People, and I assure You, by this Belt of Wampum, that there shall be no more use made of

---

[8] *Sagogsaanagechtheyky* ("the place of the name bearers"): The town of Onondaga.

it for the future, but it shall be buried. In Confirmation of what I say I give You this Belt of Wampum."

The solemn Cry, by way of thanksgiving & Joy, was repeated as many Times as there were Nations present. The Speaker then proceeded:

—4. "Brethren, the united Nations, this String of Wampum serves to bury all that unhappy accident under the Ground, and to Lay a heavy stone upon it to keep it under for Ever."

He laid down some Strings of Wampum. The usual Cry was given.

—5. "Brethren, the united Nations, these Strings of Wampum serve to dispell the Dark Cloud that overshadowed Us for some Time, that the Sun may shine again and we may be able to see one another with Pleasure."

He laid down some Strings of Wampum. The usual Cry, by way of Approbation and Thanks, was given. The Speaker proceeded:

—6. "Brethren, the united Nations, these Strings of Wampum serve to take away the Bitterness of your Spirit, and to purge You from the abundance and overflow of your Gall;[9] all wise People judge it to be a dangerous Distemper; when Men have too much of that it gives an Open Door to evil Spirits to enter in, and I cannot help believing that my Brethren, the united Nations, are often sick of that Distemper."

He laid down four Rows of Wampum; the usual Cry was given by way of Approbation; the Speaker proceeded:

—7. "Brethren, the united Nations, this String of Wampum serves to mend the Chain of Friendship again, which was lately hurt and was in danger of being broke. Let good understanding & true Friendship be restor'd and subsist among us for Ever."

Layd four Rows of Wampum, the usual Cry of approbation was given, and the Speaker proceeded:

—8. "Brethren, the United Nation, The old and wise People of my Country joined with me, and we Lodged a fine present in the hands of your Brother Onas for your Use, as a token of my own and my People's sincere Disposition to Preserve Peace and Friendship with you. We will send Commissioners to you next Spring to treat with you about the Land now in Dispute and in the Possession of my People. Let the place and Time be appointed for certain, that we may not miss one another."

---

[9]*Gall*: Feelings of bitterness, resentment, or anger.

Layd some Strings of Wampum; The usual Cry, by every Nation in Particular, was given by way of thanksgiving & Joy; the Speaker Concluded & said, "Brethren, I have no more to say at present, but only desire You to give me a Speedy Answer, I have been here many Days."

All the Wampum were hung over a Stick laid across the House about six Foot from the Ground, several Kettles of Hominy, boil'd Indian Corn & Bread was brought in by the Women, the biggest of which was set before Assariquoa by the Divider; all dined together; there was about sixty People. After Dinner they walked out, every Nation's Deputies by themselves, and soon came in again and sat together for about two hours; then Zilla Woolie proclaimed that Assaryquoa was to have an Answer now imediately; Upon which all the men in Town gather'd again, and the House was full, and many stood out of Door (so it was in the forenoon when the Message was delivered to them). Zilla Woolie desired Assaryquoa to give Ear, Tocanumtie being appointed for their Speaker, Spoke to the following Purpose: S—

"Brother Assaryquoa, the unhappy Skirmish which happen'd last Winter betwixt your People and some of our Warriours was not less surprizing to us than to You; we were very sorry to hear it; all amongst us were surprised; a Smoke arose from the bottomless Pitt, and a dark Cloud overshadow'd us; the Chain of Friendship was indanger'd & disappeared, and all was in a Confusion. We, the Chiefs of the united Nations, took hold of the Chain with all our Strength, we were resolved not to let it slip before we received a deadly Blow. But to our great Satisfaction, in the Darkest Time, our Brother Onas enter'd our Door and Offer'd his Mediation. He judged very right to become Mediator betwixt us. We were drunk on both sides, and the overflow of our Galls and the Blood that was shed had corrupted our Hearts, both Your's and our's. You did very well to come to our fire and Comfort the Mourning Families. We thank You; this Belt shall serve for the same Purpose to Comfort the Familyes in Mourning amongst You."

Laid a Belt of Wampum. After I thank'd them their Speaker proceeded:

—2. "Brother Assaryquoa, you have healed the Wounds of the Hearts of those Familys in Mourning both here & at Niharuntaquoa. We thank you kindly for your so doing. Let this Belt of Wampum have the same Effect upon your People, to heal the Wounds and Comfort them, as your's had upon our's."

Laid a Belt of Wampum, the usual thanks was given, & the Speaker proceeded:

—3. "Brother Assaryquoa, you judged very right in saying that an evil Spirit was the promoter of the late unhappy Skirmish. We do not doubt but you have by this Time full Satisfaction from your own People besides what You had from Us, that your People had begun Hostilities; but let have begun who will, we assure You it was the Spirit that dwells amongst the Catabaws, and by which they are ruled, that did it, for Brethren will never treat one another after this Manner without an Evil Spirit enters them. We agree with you and your Counsellors, the old and wise People of your Country, and disapprove the Action highly; we thank You Brother Assaryquoa for removing your Hatchet and for burying it under a heavy Stone. Let this Belt of Wampum serve to remove our Hatchet from You and not only bury it, but we will fling it into the Bottomless Pitt, into the Ocean, there shall be no more Use made of it. In Confirmation of what we say, we give You this Belt of Wampum."

After the usual Approbation was given, the Speaker proceeded:

—4. "Brother Assaryquoa, let this String of Wampum serve to heal the very mark of the Wounds, so that nothing may be seen of it after this Day, for it was done betwixt Brethren; let no more mention be made of it hereafter for ever, in Publick or Private."

Lay'd down four Strings of Wampum. The usual Cry by way of Approbation was given, and the Speaker proceeded:

—5. "Brother Assaryquoa, this String of Wampum serves to return you our Thanks for dispelling the dark Cloud that overshadow'd Us for some Time. Let the Sun shine again, let us look upon one another with Pleasure and Joy."

Lay'd some Strings of Wampum. The usual Approbation was given, and the Speaker proceeded:

—6. "Brother Assaryquoa, you have taken away the bitterness of our Spirit, and purged us from the abundance and overflow of our Gall. We judge with all the rest of the wise People, that when Men have too much of that it is like a dangerous Distemper; but it is not only your Brethren, the united Nations, that have too much Gall, but the Europeans labour likewise under that Distemper, in particular your back Inhabitants; you did very well in taking away the overflow of Gall. Let this String of Wampum serve to purge your People also from the overflow of their Gall, and to remove the bitterness of their Spirit; also, we own it to be very necessary on both sides. We thank You for the good advice."

Laid four Rows of Wampum. The usual approbation was given, and the Speaker proceeded:

—7. "Brother Assaryquoa, this String of Wampum serves to thank you for mending the Chain of Friendship which was lately hurt and in danger; we agree with you very readily. Let good understanding & true Friendship be restored and subsist among us for Ever."

Laid four Rows of Wampum. The usual approbation was given, and the Speaker proceeded:

—8. "Brother Assaryquoa, we thank you kindly for the present you and the Old and Wise of your Country lodged in the Hands of our Brother Onas, your good Friend, as a token of your sincere Disposition to preserve Peace and Friendship with Us. Let this String of Wampum serve to assure you of the like good Disposition towards you and your People, and as an assurance that we will come down within the Borders of Pennsylvania to a place called Canadagueany,[10] next Spring, and we will be very glad of seeing your Commissioners there, we will treat them as becomes Brethren with good Chear and Pleasure. We will set out from our several Towns after eight Moons are past by, when the ninth just is to be seen, this present Moon, which is almost expired, not to be reckoned, Upon which you may Depend; in Confirmation whereof, we give you this String of Wampum."

The usual Approbation being given, the Speaker proceeded:

—"Brother Assaryquoa, we have no more to say at present, but we will not permit you to Leave Us yet, but stay a Day or two longer with us. We have just now received Intelligence that the Jonontowas[11] are on the Road with some of the Cherikees' Deputies in order to strike a Peace with Us; They, the Cherikees, hindred the Jonontowas from coming sooner, and you will then hear the Particulars."

Then the Speaker directed his Discourse to the Deputies of the Nanticokes, who had been there all along present, and said: "Brethren, the Nanticokes, We desire you will prepare for to-morrow and deliver your Message to us; and as you have neither the united Nations, their Tongue nor Ear, we have thought fit to hear you speak with our English Ear, and to speak to you with our English Tongue. There is the Man (pointing to me) who is the Guardian of all the Indians." I was desired to acquaint the Nanticokes with it, which I did, and

---

[10] *Canadagueany* (Conodoguinet): An abandoned Indian town on the west side of the Susquehanna River across from modern Harrisburg.

[11] *Jonontowas* (Jenontowanos, *tionontowa:neh ononh,* "great hill people"): Senecas. Fenton, *Great Law,* 436.

they were well pleased. They could talk some English, but not one word of the united Nation's Language.

The 1st of August, the Nanticokes spoke, and had their Answer the same Day; the whole day was spent about it.

The 2d, the Council of the united Nation met again, and Zillawoolie desired me to give my Attendance, and take Notice of what should be said to put it down in Writing immediately, and with Particular Care he spoke as follows: "Brother Onas, Assaryquoa, and the Governor of Maryland: We are ingaged in a Warr with the Catabaws which will last to the End of the World, for they molest Us and speak Contemptuously of Us, which our Warriours will not bear, and they will soon go to War against them again; it will be in vain for Us to diswade them from it. We desire you, by this String of Wampum, to publish it amongst your back Inhabitants to be of good behaviour to our Warriors, and look upon them as their Brethren, that we may never have such a Dangerous Breach hereafter. We give you the strongest Assurance that we will use our best Endeavour to perswade and charge them to be of good Behaviour every where amongst our Brethren the English, with whom we are one body and Soul, one Heart and one Head, for what has happened is no more to be seen, and no token or mark remains thereof. Let the Spirit of the Catawba's be banished away from Us which will set Brethren to fall out; Let Treaties of Friendship be observed, and believe no Lies.

"Our Brother Onas knows very well that some Years ago we made a new Road on the outside of your Inhabitants, tho' they had seated themselves down upon our Land, now your People seated themselves down again upon the new Road and shut it up, and there is no more room for a new Road because of the Terrible Mountains full of Stones and no game there, so that the Road cannot be removed. To inforce this upon You, we give you this String of Wampum, which serves likewise for an Assurance that we will observe Treaties of Friendship with You and believe no Lies, and will perswade our Warriors to behave very well every where amongst your People our Brethren."

Laid a String of Wampum of three Rows—they desired that this might be sent to Maryland and Virginia immediately, from Philadelphia.

"Brother Onas, this String of Wampum serves to return you our Hearty thanks for your Kind Mediation. We thank our Brother Assaryquoa for the Kind visit. Let good Friendship and Peace be amongst Us to the End of the World."

After all was over, according to the Ancient Custom of that Fire, a Song of Friendship and Joy was sung by the Chiefs, after this the Council Fire on their side was put out. I with the same Ceremonee put out the Fire on behalf of Assaryquoa & Onas, and they departed.

The 3d of August I put down, in the Morning, the Speech of the Nanticokes and visited Tocammtie. All the Chiefs of the Onondagoes came to see Us—took my Leave of them—set out about nine and departed from Onondago. They desired to be remembred to their Brethren in Philadelphia, in Particular to the Governor and James Logan.[12]

The time that We staid at Onondagoe we were well entertain'd with Hominy, Venison, Dryed Eels, Squashes, and Indian Corn bread. They gave Us provision on the Road homeward, so much as we wanted. We passed Cajadachse—took my Leave thereof—Zillawoolie and I arrived that Day on the first Branch of Sasquehannah.

[12]*Logan*: (1674–1751) The Penn family's agent in the province during the first four decades of the eighteenth century, a member of the Provincial Council, a prominent merchant, and a major figure in the colony's relations with Indians.

4

WITHAM MARSHE

Journal of the Treaty Held with the Six Nations

June–July 1744

The minutes of the Lancaster Treaty that Benjamin Franklin published focus almost exclusively on the official proceedings, but every diplomatic encounter between Indians and colonists had much more going on behind the scenes (or, as Iroquois put it, "in the bushes" away from the light of the "council fire"). Fortunately, Witham Marshe (?–1765), a young gentleman from Scotland who served as secretary to the Maryland

"Witham Marshe's Journal of the Treaty Held with the Six Nations by the Commissioners of Maryland, and Other Provinces, at Lancaster, in Pennsylvania, June, 1744," *Collections of the Massachusetts Historical Society*, 1st Series, Volume 7 (Boston: Samuel Hall, 1801), 171–201.

Treaty Commissioners, not only took part in the council's formal and informal encounters, but he also kept a lively, colorful journal giving his impressions of Indians and colonists alike. Compare his day-by-day account with Franklin's (Part Two): Where do they overlap, where do they differ, and why? How good an observer of Iroquois was Marshe? Of colonists? Though Marshe polished his diary after the official minutes appeared, he never published it, leaving us to wonder what purpose and what audience he had in mind when he wrote.

Thursday [June 21, 1744], *P. M.* . . . We were informed that the Indians would not arrive till to-morrow, they marching very slow, occasioned by their having a great many small children and old men.

Messrs. Calvert, Craddock and myself went into, and viewed the court-house of this town.[1] It is a pretty large brick building, two stories high. The ground room, where the justices of this county hold their court, is very spacious. There is a handsome bench, and railed in, whereon they sit, and a chair in the midst of it, which is filled by the judge. Below this bench, is a large table, of half oval form; round this, and under their Worships, sit the county clerk, and the several attornies of the court. . . . There are particular seats and places allotted to the sheriff, crier, &c.

Fronting the justices' bench, and on each side of it, are several long steps, or stairs, raised each above the other, like the steps leading into the north door of St. Paul's.[2] On these steps, stand the several auditors and spectators, when a court is held here. It was on these, that the Indian chiefs sat, when they treated with the several governments. This court-house is capable to contain above 800 persons, without incommoding each other.

When we had surveyed this room, we went up stairs, into one over head. This is a good room, and has a large chimney. In this the justices sit in the month of February, for the convenience of the fire. Adjoining to this room, is a smaller one, where the juries are kept to agree on their verdict.

---

[1]*Benedict Calvert* (c. 1724–1788): Calvert and Rev. Thomas Craddock were part of the Maryland entourage. Calvert was the illegitimate son of Charles Calvert, the 5th Lord Baltimore and Proprietor of Maryland. Edward C. Papenfuse et al., eds., *A Biographical Dictionary of the Maryland Legislature, 1635–1789*, Studies in Maryland History and Culture (Baltimore: Johns Hopkins University Press, 1979–1985), I, 184–85.

[2]*St. Paul's*: St. Paul's Cathedral in London.

On the top of the court-house is a kind of cupola. We ascended a ladder, and got into it. From hence we had a complete view of the whole town, and the country several miles round, and likewise of part of Susquehannah river, at twelve miles distance. . . .

Friday, June 22d, 1744. . . .
The Indian chiefs not being yet come, we had no business to do.

The honourable the commissioners of Virginia gave our commissioners, and the several Maryland gentlemen, an invitation to dine with them in the court-house, which we did, betwixt one and two. During our dinner, the deputies of the Six Nations, with their followers and attendants, to the number of 252, arrived in town. Several of their squaws, or wives, with some small children, rode on horseback, which is very unusual with them. They brought their fire-arms and bows and arrows, as well as tomahawks. A great concourse of people followed them. They marched in very good order, with *Cannasateego*, one of the Onondago chiefs, at their head; who, when he came near to the court-house wherein we were dining, sung, in the Indian language, a song, inviting us to a renewal of all treaties heretofore made, and that now is to be made.

Mr. Weiser, the interpreter, who is highly esteemed by the Indians, and is one of their council of state, (though a German by birth) conducted them to some vacant lots in the back part of the town, where sundry poles and boards were placed. Of these, and some boughs of trees from the woods, the Indians made *wigwams*, or cabins, wherein they resided during the treaty. They will not, on any occasion whatsoever, dwell, or even stay, in houses built by white people.[3]

They placed their cabins according to the rank each nation of them holds in their grand council. The *Onondagoes* nation was placed on the right hand and upper end; then the others, according to their several dignities.

After dining, and drinking the loyal healths,[4] all the younger gentlemen of Virginia, Maryland, and Pennsylvania, went with Mr. Conrad Weiser to the Indian camp, where they had erected their several cabins. We viewed them all, and heartily welcomed *Cannasateego*, and

---

[3] *They will not . . . white people*: Marshe here reveals his inexperience with Indians and with treaties. In fact, natives frequently lodged in colonial houses, during councils and at other times.

[4] *loyal healths*: Toasting the king and the royal family was customary at formal dinners throughout the British Empire.

Tachanuntie, (alias the Black Prince) two chiefs of the Onondagoes, to town. They shaked us by the hands, and seemed very well pleased with us. I gave them some snuff, for which they returned me thanks in their language.

The first of these sachems (or chiefs) was a tall, well-made man; had a very full chest, and brawny limbs. He had a manly countenance, mixed with a good-natured smile. He was about 60 years of age; very active, strong, and had a surprising liveliness in his speech, which I observed in the discourse betwixt him, Mr. Weiser, and some of the sachems.

Tachanuntie, another sachem, or chief of the same nation, was a tall, thin man; old, and not so well featured as Cannasateego: I believe he may be near the same age with him. He is one of the greatest warriors that ever the Five Nations produced, and has been a great war-captain for many years past [see Figure 6].

He is also called *the Black Prince*, because, as I was informed, he was either begotten on an Indian woman by a negro, or by an Indian chief on some negro woman; but by which of the two, I could not be well assured.[5]

The Governor of Canada, (whom these Indians call *Onantio*) will not treat with any of the Six Nations of Indians, unless *Tachanuntie* is personally present, he having a great sway in all the Indian councils.

Our interpreter, Mr. Weiser desired us, whilst we were here, not to talk much of the Indians, nor laugh at their dress, or make any remarks on their behaviour: if we did, it would be very much resented by them, and might cause some differences to arise betwixt the white people and them. Besides, most of them understood English, though they will not speak it when they are in treaty.

The Indians, in general, were poorly dressed, having old match coats,[6] and those ragged; few, or no shirts, and those they had, as black as the Scotchman made the *Jamaicans*, when he wrote in his letter they were as black as that ● blot.

When they had rested some little space of time, several of them began to paint themselves with divers sorts of colours, which ren-

---

[5]*He is also called . . . well assured*: Another source suggests a different reason for the name: "His chest was literally black with a network of devices and designs, tattooed into the skin with gunpowder." William M. Beauchamp, ed, *Moravian Journals Relating to Central New York, 1745–1766* (Syracuse, N.Y.: The Dehler Press, 1916), 20.

[6]*match coat*: A loose-fitting coat or cloak commonly worn by Native Americans in eastern North America, usually made of coarse wool or cloth.

dered them frightful. Some of the others rubbed bear's grease on their faces, and then laid upon that a white paint. When we had made a sufficient survey of them and their cabins, we went to the court-house, where the Indians were expected to meet the Governor of Pennsylvania, the Hon. GEORGE THOMAS, Esq. and to be by him congratulated on their arrival at this town.

Friday, P. M. Between 5 and 6 o'clock, Mr. Weiser accompanied the several Indian chiefs from their camp up to the court-house, which they entered and seated themselves after their own manner. Soon after, his Honour the Governor, the honourable the commissioners of Virginia, the honourable the commissioners of Maryland, and the young gentlemen from the three governments, went into the court-house to the Indians. There the Governor, and all the commissioners, severally welcomed the Indians to Lancaster, and shaked hands with the sachems.

Then his Honour seated himself in the chair on the bench, the Virginia commissioners placed themselves, *to wit*, the Hon. Col. Thomas Lee, and Col. William Beverly, on his right hand, and our honourable commissioners on his left. William Peters,[7] Esq. secretary of Pennsyl-

---

[7] *William Peters*: William Peters was more likely Richard Peters (see "Major Figures in the Lancaster Treaty of 1744"), who was indeed provincial secretary and the principal scribe at the treaty.

Opposite: **Figure 6**   *"The Brave Old Hendrick"*
No portrait of Canassatego or any of the other Iroquois at Lancaster in 1744 has survived—if any was ever made. Only the written descriptions by Marshe offer an image of these ambassadors. This 1755 engraving, however, suggests what an Iroquois diplomat of that era looked like. It claims to depict the Mohawk leader Hendrick (whom Conrad Weiser, Pennsylvania Indian agent and adopted Mohawk, knew as Henery Dyionoagon). Hendrick was not at Lancaster in the summer of 1744—he was then heading a Mohawk delegation to a council in Boston, Massachusetts, where he and his party wore "laced hats . . . laced matchcoats, and ruffled shirts." The fine English clothing, like the presents colonial officials bestowed upon Six Nations leaders at the conclusion of the Lancaster Treaty in 1744, was visible testimony to the native's alliance to the British Empire. It also demonstrated for all to see his ability to acquire English goods, a vital element for any headman, who was expected to redistribute valuable commodities to his people. The tomahawk in one hand and the wampum string in the other symbolize his willingness to make peace or war.
Courtesy of the John Carter Brown Library at Brown University.

vania, sat in the middle of the table, under the Governor, and Mr. William Black, secretary to the Virginia commissioners, on his right hand, and myself, as secretary to the commissioners of Maryland, on his left hand.

The Governor desired the interpreter to tell the Indians, "He was very glad to see them here, and should not trouble them with business this day, but desired they would rest themselves, after their great journey." This, Mr. Weiser interpreted to them, whereat they seemed well enough pleased, and made the Governor a suitable answer.

When this was done, a good quantity of punch, wine, and pipes and tobacco, were given to the sachems, and the Governor and all the commissioners drank to them, whom they pledged. When they had smoked some small time, and each drank a glass or two of wine and punch, they retired to their cabins. . . .

Saturday, June 23d, 1744, at Lancaster.

This day I was seized with a lax,[8] and small fever, occasioned by drinking the water of this town. . . .

All this day the Indians staid in their wigwams; and it is usual for them to rest two days after their journey, before they treat, or do business with the English.

After supper, this evening, I went with Mr. President Logan's son,[9] and divers other young gentlemen, to the Indians' camp, they being then dancing one of their lighter war dances.[10]

They performed it after this manner: Thirty or forty of the younger men formed themselves into a ring, a fire being lighted (notwithstanding the excessive heat) and burning clear in the midst of them. Near this, sat three elderly Indians, who beat a drum to the time of the others' dancing. Then the dancers hopped round the ring, after a frantic fashion, not unlike the priests of Bacchus[11] in old times, and repeated, sundry times, these sounds, *Yohoh! Bugh!* Soon after this, the major part of the dancers (or rather hoppers) set up a horrid shriek or halloo!

---

[8]*lax*: Probably diarrhea.

[9]*Mr. President Logan's son*: William Logan (1718–1777), son of James Logan, the Penn family's agent in the province.

[10]*war dances*: It is unlikely that Indians would perform a war dance during peace talks. This was probably "Standing Quiver," a stomp dance. William N. Fenton, *The Great Law and the Longhouse: A Political History of the Iroquois Confederacy* (Norman: University of Oklahoma Press, 1998), 426.

[11]*Bacchus*: The Greek god of wine.

They continued dancing and hopping, after this manner, several hours, and rested very seldom. Once, whilst I staid with them, they did rest themselves; immediately thereupon, the three old men began to sing an Indian song, the tune of which was not disagreeable to the white by-standers. Upon this, the young warriors renewed their terrible shriek and halloo, and formed themselves into a ring, environing the three old ones, and danced as before. Mr. Calvert, myself, and some others slipped through the dancers, and stood near the fire; and when the drum-beaters ceased their noise, we shaked them by the hand. Here we presented some clean pipes to them, which were very acceptable, most of the Indians being great smokers of tobacco. A *Conestogoe*, or *Susquehannah* Indian,[12] stood without the circle, and importuned the white by-standers to give money to the young children, which was done. Whilst this diversion happened, some High-Dutch,[13] belonging to the town, brought their guns with them to the camp; which being perceived by the *Conestogoe*, he informed us, it would be very displeasing to the Indians, who would resent it, though brought thither with ever so innocent an intent; therefore desired us to tell the Germans to withdraw, and leave their musquets out of their sight, otherwise some bad consequences might ensue. We complied with his request, and made the Germans retire.

From the camp I went to Worrall's [Inn], and sat up till eleven o'clock; to whose house I heard the Indian drum, and the warriors repeating their terrible noise and dancing; and at this sport of theirs, they continued till near one in the morning.

These young men are surprisingly agile, strong, and straight limbed. They shoot, both with the gun and bow and arrow, most dexterously. They likewise throw their tomahawk (or little hatchet) with great certainty, at an indifferent large object, for twenty or thirty yards distance. This weapon they use against their enemies, when they have spent their powder and ball, and destroy many of them with it.

Their chiefs, who were deputed to treat with the English by their different nations, were very sober men, which is rare for an Indian to be so, if he can get liquor. They behaved very well, during our stay amongst them, and sundry times refused drinking in a moderate way. When ever they renew old treaties of friendship, or make any bargain about lands they sell to the English, they take great care to abstain

---

[12] *Susquehannah Indian*: Conestogas, one of the "props" to the Iroquois Longhouse, lived among colonists on a reservation near Lancaster.

[13] *High-Dutch*: "Deutsch," or German colonists.

from intoxicating drink, for fear of being over-reached; but when they have finished their business, then some of them will drink without measure.

Sunday, June 24th, 1744. . . .

In the evening, walked to the Indian camp, where they were dancing in the manner described last night, only the number of dancers was augmented, they having taken in several small boys, to make a larger ring.

Betwixt 8 and 9, this night, supped with my brother secretary, Mr. Black, in his lodgings at Mr. George Sanderson's. We had pleasant company, good wine, and lime-punch. From hence I went to Worrall's. . . . I rested well, . . . but this happened by my giving orders to my landlord's servants, this morning, to wash our room with cold water, and take my bed from its bedstead, and lay it on the floor; and by this means the bugs and fleas were defeated of their prey.

Monday morning, 25th *June,* 1744.

At 10 o'clock, the Indian sachems met the Governor, the honourable commissioners of Virginia, and those of this province [Maryland], when his Honour made them a speech, to which Cannasateego returned an answer in behalf of all the others present.

The Indians staid in the court-house about two hours; and were regaled with some bumbo and sangree.[14]

The honourable commissioners from Virginia and Maryland dined in the court-house, as did the gentlemen of both governments; we had two tables, and a great variety of victuals; our company being about thirty in number.

In the court-house, Monday, P. M.

The Governor, and all the honourable commissioners, resumed their several seats here; and then the chiefs came in, and took their places.

Edmund Jenings,[15] Esq. as first commissioner for Maryland, made a speech to the Six Nations, which was interpreted to them by Mr.

---

[14]*bumbo:* A drink made from rum, water, sugar, and nutmeg; *sangree* (Sangria): A Spanish red wine, often mixed with lemonade or a sweetener.

[15]*Edmund Jenings* (Jennings; ?–1756): A leading Maryland official who was then a member of the Provincial Council. Papenfuse et al., eds., *Biographical Dictionary of the Maryland Legislature,* II, 487–88.

Weiser. Whilst Mr. Jenings delivered his speech, he gave the interpreter a string and two belts of wampum, which were by him presented to the sachem Cannasateego; and the Indians thereupon gave the cry of approbation; by this we were sure the speech was well approved by the Indians. This cry is usually made on presenting wampum to the Indians in a treaty, and is performed thus: The grand chief and speaker amongst them pronounces the word *jo-hah!* with a loud voice, singly; then all the others join in this sound, *woh!* dwelling some little while upon it, and keeping exact time with each other, and immediately, with a sharp noise and force, utter this sound, *wugh!* This is performed in great order, and with the utmost ceremony and decorum; and with the Indians is like our English huzza!

Monday evening, in the court-house chamber.

I supped with the Governor, the honourable commissioners, and the gentlemen of Philadelphia, who attended his Honour to this town. We had an elegant entertainment; and after supper the Governor was extremely merry, and thereby set an example of agreeable mirth, which ran through the whole company. During this merriment, two Germans happened to pass by the court-house with a harp and fiddle, and played some tunes under the window of our room: upon that, they were ordered to come up stairs, where the Governor required them to divert us, which they did, but not with the harmony of their music, (for that was very uncouth and displeasing to us, who had heard some of the best hands in England) but by playing a tune, of some sort, to a young Indian, who danced a jig with Mr. Andrew Hamilton,[16] in a most surprising manner. At nine o'clock, the Governor and commissioners left us; and then the younger persons raised their jollity by dancing in the Indian dress, and after their manner.

Tuesday, 26th June. . . .

We dined in the court-house; and soon after I received orders from the above commissioner [Jenings], to acquaint all the Maryland gentlemen, "That they should desist going into the court-house this afternoon, during our treaty with the Six Nations." Pursuant to which order, I informed the gentlemen of our commissioners' pleasure, at which the first were much disgusted, as were the Virginia gentlemen, who had the same commands laid on them by the secretary of their commissioners.

---

[16]*Andrew Hamilton* (?–1747): The son of a prominent lawyer and provincial official who held office and was a merchant.

Five o'clock, P. M. His Honour the Governor of Pennsylvania, and the honourable the commissioners of Virginia and Maryland, met the Indian chiefs in the court-house, when Cannasateego answered our speech of yesterday, and presented a string and two belts of wampum: which being done, the further execution of the treaty was adjourned until the next day.

By order of our commissioners, and at the request of Mr. Weiser, the interpreter, I bought half a gross of tobacco pipes, to be presented to the Indians at their camp; which was accordingly done, and they seemed well pleased at the gift, such pipes being scarce with them.

Wednesday, 27th June. . . .

P. M. 5 o'clock. The Governor and, all the honourable commissioners, again met, and treated with the Six Nations, in the court-house, when Tachanuntie, the famous Black Prince, . . . answered the speech made yesterday by the Hon. Col. Lee, one of the Virginia commissioners; and in token that it was well received and approved by the chiefs, Tachanuntie presented one string and two belts of wampum to his Majesty's commissioners of Virginia. Then Mr. Commissioner Jenings desired the interpreter to ask the Indians if they would be ready for a conference to-morrow morning, in the court-house chamber, with the commissioners of Maryland; which he did, and the Indians answered, that they would meet for that purpose, as desired.

At 8 o'clock, this evening, I went, with three of our honourable commissioners, to a ball in the court-house chamber; to which his Honour the Governor of Pennsylvania, the commissioners of Virginia and Maryland, and the gentlemen of the several colonies, with sundry inhabitants of this town, were invited.

James Hamilton, Esq. the proprietor of Lancaster,[17] made the ball, and opened it, by dancing two minuets with two of the ladies here, which last danced wilder time than any Indians.

Our music and musicians were the same as described last Monday evening.

The females (I dare not call them ladies, for that would be a profanation of the name) were, in general, very disagreeable. The dancers

---

[17] *Lancaster*: In 1735 James Hamilton (1710–1783) acquired from his father and from the Penn family the lands on which Lancaster would stand, making him the town's "Proprietor." Jerome H. Wood Jr., *Conestoga Crossroads: Lancaster, Pennsylvania, 1730–1790* (Harrisburg: Pennsylvania Historical and Museum Commission, 1979), 3–5, 33.

consisted of Germans and Scotch-Irish; but there were some Jew-esses, who had not long since come from New-York, that made a toler-able appearance, being well dressed, and of an agreeable behaviour.

There was a large and elegant supper prepared in the court-house chamber, of which the Governor, some of the honourable commission-ers, and the female dancers, first eat; then the other gentlemen in order, and afterwards the younger gentlemen. The dances were con-cluded about 12 o'clock; but myself, with several others of the younger sort, staid till after one in the morning.

Thursday, 28th of June, 1744, *A. M.*

At 9 this morning, the commissioners of Maryland and the Six Nations met in the court-house chamber, according to agreement of yesterday.

Here we opened the several bales and boxes of goods, to be pre-sented the Indians, they having been bought at Philadelphia, and sent hither for that end.

Before the chiefs viewed and handled the several goods, Mr. Com-missioner Jenings made them a speech in the name of the Governor of Maryland, with which, after it was interpreted to them by Mr. Weiser, they seemed well pleased.

The chiefs turned over, and narrowly inspected the goods, and asked the prices of them; which being told them, they seemed some-what dissatisfied; and desired to go down into the court-house, to con-sult among themselves, (which is their usual method, if it concerns any matter of importance, as this was, for they must give a particular account of their whole negotiation to their several tribes, when they return) with their interpreter. They did so; and after some time came up again, and agreed with our commissioners to release their claim and right to any lands now held by the inhabitants of Maryland, and for which the said Indians were not heretofore satisfied. . . .

The . . . goods were accordingly given the Indians, as agreed on by both parties; after which, our commissioners ordered me to go to Mr. Worrall, and desire him to send some punch for the sachems, which was accordingly done; and after they had severally drank health to the commissioners, and the compliment returned by the latter, the Indians retired to their wigwams, and the honourable commissioners went to their lodgings about 12 o'clock.

Post Meridiem. The commissioners of Virginia had a private treaty with the chiefs, in the court-house, when Col. Lee made them a speech. . . .

In the evening, about 7 o'clock, I accompanied my friend, Col. Nathan Rigbie,[18] to the Indian cabins, where, having collected several of their papooses (or little children) together, he flung a handful of English half-pennies amongst them, for which they scrambled heartily, and with the utmost earnestness. This pleased the elder sort very much; and they esteem it a great mark of friendship, if the white people make presents to their children, or treat them with any particular notice. I gave the papooses some small beads, which were kindly received. The young men, this night, again danced a war-dance, as described on Saturday last; at which were present a great number of white people. When the colonel and myself had taken a view of the Onondagoes', Cahugas' and Senecas' cabins, he went from me to the ring of dancers, and then I went to a cabin, where I heard the celebrated Mrs. Montour,[19] a French lady, (but now, by having lived so long among the Six Nations, is become almost an Indian) had her residence. When I approached the wigwam, I saluted her in French, and asked her whether she was not born in Canada? of what parents? and whether she had not lived a long time with the Indians? She answered me in the same language very civilly, and after some compliments were passed betwixt us, told me, in a polite manner, "That she was born in Canada, whereof her father (who was a French gentleman) had been Governor; under whose administration, the then Five Nations of Indians had made war against the French, and the Hurons in that government, (whom we term the French Indians, from espousing their part against the English, and living in Canada) and that, in the war, she was taken by some of the Five Nations' warriors, being then about ten years of age; and by them was carried away into their country, where she was habited and brought up in the same manner as their children: That when she grew up to years of maturity, she was married to a famous war captain of those nations, who was in great esteem for the glory he procured in the wars he carried on against the Catawbas, a great nation of Indians to the south-west of Virginia, by whom she had several children; but about fifteen years ago, he was killed in a battle with them; since which, she has not been married: That she had little or no remembrance of the place of her birth, nor

---

[18]*Nathan Rigbie*: Nathaniel Rigbie was with the Maryland delegation to the treaty. His son, Nathaniel Rigbie Jr., was also there.

[19]*Mrs. Montour* (Elisabeth or Isabelle Couc, 1667–c. 1752): A renowned frontier figure who was an emissary among the French, English, Iroquois, and other native peoples.

indeed of her parents, it being near fifty years since she was ravished[20] from them by the Indians."

She has been a handsome woman, genteel, and of polite address,
notwithstanding her residence has been so long among the Indians;
though formerly she was wont to accompany the several chiefs, who
used to renew treaties of friendship with the proprietor and governor
of Pennsylvania, at Philadelphia, the metropolis of that province; and
being a white woman, was there very much caressed by the gentle-
women of that city, with whom she used to stay for some time. She
retains her native language, by conversing with the Frenchmen who
trade for fur, skins, &c. among the six nations; and our language she
learned at Philadelphia, as likewise of our traders, who go back into
the Indians' country. In her cabin were two of her daughters, by the
war-captain, who were both married to persons of the same station,
and were then gone to war with the Catawbas before mentioned. One
of these young women had a son, about five years old, who, I think,
was one of the finest featured and limbed children mine eyes ever
saw, and was not so tawny, or greased, as the other Indian children
were; but, on the contrary, his cheeks were ruddy, mixed with a deli-
cate white, had eyes and hair of an hazel colour, and was neatly
dressed in a green ban-jan,[21] and his other garments were suitable.

Madame Montour has but one son,[22] who, for his prowess and mar-
tial exploits, was lately made a captain, and a member of the Indian
council, and is now gone to war against the Catawbas, with her son-
in-law.

She is in great esteem with the best sort of white people, and by
them always treated with abundance of civility; and whenever she
went to Philadelphia, (which formerly she did pretty often) the ladies
of that city always invited her to their houses, entertained her well,
and made her several presents.

From this cabin, when I had taken leave of Mrs. Montour and her
daughters, I returned to the dancers, who were continuing their
mirth; and afterwards returned to my lodgings.

---

[20] *ravished*: Kidnapped.

[21] *ban-jan* (Banyan): "A loose coat ending just above or below the knees" and fastened in front with a clasp, buttons, or hooks. C. Willett Cunnington and Phillis Cunnington, *Handbook of English Costume in the Eighteenth Century* (London: Faber and
Faber Limited, 1957), 73–74.

[22] *son*: Andrew Montour (?–1772) was, like his mother, an important go-between.

Friday, June the 29th, 1744, A. M.

Our commissioners and the Six Nations had a private conference in the court-house chamber, when they jointly proceeded to settle the bounds and quantity of land the latter were to release to Lord Baltimore, in Maryland; but the Indians, not very well apprehending our commissioners, in their demand respecting the bounds of the lands to be released, occasioned a great delay in the finishing of that business; however, it was wholly settled in the afternoon, upon Mr. Weiser's conference with the Governor of Pennsylvania, his Majesty's commissioners of Virginia, and those of Maryland, and also with the Indians in council, where he debated the matter more fully; and explained our commissioners' demands in so clear a manner, that they came to such an amicable determination, as proved agreeable to each party. We again presented the sachems, here, with bumbo punch, with which they drank prosperity and success to their Father, the great King over the waters, and to the healths of our commissioners.

This day we dined at our landlord Worrall's; and it was agreed, by the commissioners of Maryland, to invite all the Six Nations' chiefs, to dine with them, in company with the Governor and Virginia commissioners, to-morrow, in the court-house; against which time, orders were given to prepare a large and elegant entertainment. . . .

Saturday, 30th June, 1744, A. M. . . .

At ten, his Majesty's commissioners had a conference with the Indians in the court-house chamber, to which no other persons than themselves were admitted.

One o'clock, P. M. The twenty-four chiefs of the Six Nations, by invitation of yesterday from the honourable commissioners of Maryland, dined with them in the court-house; when were present, at other tables, his Honour the Governor of Pennsylvania, the honourable commissioners of Virginia, and a great many gentlemen of the three colonies. There were a large number of the inhabitants of Lancaster likewise present to see the Indians dine.

We had five tables, great variety of dishes, and served up in very good order. The sachems sat at two separate tables; at the head of one, the famous orator, Cannasateego, sat, and the others were placed according to their rank. As the Indians are not accustomed to eat in the same manner as the English, or other polite nations do, we, who were secretaries on this affair, with Mr. Thomas Cookson,[23] prothonotary[24]

---

[23] *Cookson* (1710–1753): A prominent local leader.
[24] *prothonotary*: Clerk of a court.

of Lancaster county, William Logan, Esq. son of Mr. President Logan, and Mr. Nathaniel Rigbie, of Baltimore county, in Maryland, carved the meat for them, served them with cider and wine, mixed with water, and regulated the economy of the two tables. The chiefs seemed prodigiously pleased with their feast, for they fed lustily, drank heartily, and were very greasy before they finished their dinner, for, by the bye, they made no use of their forks. The interpreter, Mr. Weiser, stood betwixt the table, where the governor sat, and that, at which the sachems were placed, who, by order of his Honour, was desired to inform the Indians he drank their healths, which he did; whereupon they gave the usual cry of approbation, and returned the compliment, by drinking health to his Honour and the several commissioners. . . .

[Marshe describes the Iroquois naming ceremony for Maryland's governor, copying Gachradodon's speech and Maryland's reply from the printed treaty. As the ritual came to a close,] Mr. Weiser . . . was ordered to acquaint them, that the governor and the commissioners were then preparing to drink his Majesty's health; all which was done, and the chiefs expressed a sincere joy by their cry of approbation, and drank the same in bumpers of Madeira wine.[25] The governor, commissioners, and indeed all the persons present, except the Indians, gave three several huzzas, after the English manner, on drinking the King's health; which a good deal surprised them, they having never before heard the like noise.

Upon ending the ceremony of drinking healths, the governor and commissioners retired some little time; but within an hour, the commissioners of Virginia and Maryland entered the court-house, and afterwards went up into the chamber, as likewise the several chiefs, Mr. Weiser, and a great many of the young gentlemen. Here, by order of our commissioners, I produced the . . . release for the lands, with the seals fixed. We were obliged to put about the glass pretty briskly; and then Mr. Weiser interpreted the contents of it to the sachems, who, conferring amongst themselves about the execution of it, the major part of them seemed very inclinable to sign and deliver it; but upon Shukelemy, an Oneydoe chief's remonstrance, some of the others, with himself, refused, for that day, executing it; which refusal of Shukelemy, we imputed, and that not without reason, to some sinister and under-hand means, made use of by the Pennsylvanians, to

---

[25] *bumpers*: "A cup or glass of wine, etc., filled to the brim, *esp.* when drunk as a toast" (*Oxford English Dictionary*); *Madeira wine*: Wine from the island of Madeira, some 350 miles off the coast of Africa.

induce the sachems not to give up their right to the lands by deed, without having a larger consideration given them, by the province of Maryland, than what was specified in the release. Shukelemy, who before, we had esteemed one of our fastest friends, put us under a deep surprise and confusion, by his unfair behaviour; yet we, in some measure, extricated ourselves out of them, by the honest Cannasateego's, and the other sachems, to the number of sixteen, delivering the deed after the forms customary with the English, to which there were a great many gentlemen signed their names as witnesses. Mr. Weiser assured the commissioners, that he, with Cannasateego and some other chiefs, would so effectually represent the unfair dealing of Shukelemy, and his partisans in council, that he did not doubt to induce him and them totally to finish this business on Monday next, maugre[26] all the insinuations and misrepresentations agitated by the enemies of Maryland; and indeed Mr. Interpreter proved successful, as is evident in the transactions of Monday, and may be seen in the printed treaty.

Monday, July the 2d, 1744, *A. M.*

The honourable commissioners of Maryland, with Mr. Weiser, met at the house of George Sanderson, in this town, when the several chiefs, who had not signed the deed of release, and renunciation of their claim to lands in Maryland, did now cheerfully, and without any hesitation, execute the same, in the presence of the commissioners, and Mr. Weiser; which latter they caused to sign and deliver it on behalf of a nation not present,[27] both with his Indian name of Tarachiawagon,[28] and that of Weiser. Thus we happily effected the purchase of the lands in Maryland, by the dexterous management of the interpreter, notwithstanding the storm on Saturday, that threatened to blast our measures; and hereby gained not only some hundred thousand acres of land to Lord Baltimore, who had no good right to them before this release, but an undisturbed and quiet enjoyment of them to the several possessors, who, in fact, had bought of that Lord's agent. . . .

In the afternoon, the honourable commissioners of Virginia had a conference with the Indians in the court-house chamber, when a deed,

---

[26]*maugre*: In spite of.

[27]*nation not present*: The absent nation was the Mohawks. Weiser was an adopted member of that nation.

[28]*Tarachiawagon* ("Holder of the Heavens"): The name of an Iroquois deity.

in the nature of ours, releasing their claim to a large quantity of land, lying in that colony, was produced by Mr. Weiser to the sachems for execution, which was signed and delivered by them in the presence of divers gentlemen of the three colonies, who were witnesses to the same. Wine and sangree was presented to the chiefs, who drank to the continuation of the friendship betwixt them, and his Majesty's subjects in Virginia. After the deed was executed, Cannasateego commanded the young Indian men, then present, to entertain the Governor and commissioners, in the evening, with a particular dance, according to the custom of their nations; which was complied with about 8 o'clock. Before they performed the dance, I went to their camp, where I saw the young warriors paint themselves in a frightful manner, and on their heads place a great quantity of feathers. They took arrows and tomahawks in their hands, and then unanimously ran out of their camp, hallooing and shrieking (which was terrible to us, being strangers) up the street to Mr. Cookson's, where the Governor was; and there they made a ring, a person being placed in it, and danced round him to a horrid noise, made by the inclosed person, and the others. In this manner they continued some time, flourishing their weapons, and striving to destroy him in the ring. When they had acted thus about seven or eight minutes, then their captain ran before them, very swift, to another place, about twenty or thirty yards distance from Mr. Cookson's, and there acted the same over again. This was a representation of the Indians besieging a fort of their enemies, (who have no cannon) the person in the midst of the circle representing the fort besieged, and the Indians encircling him, the besiegers: and as it happens sometimes, that they are beaten from a fort when besieging it, so their running away, as described above, was the manner of their retreat. As soon as the Indians recovered their fatigue, they renewed the attack of the supposed fort. When they had finished the siege, and the Governor and commissioners had treated them with sangree, they immediately retired to their wigwams.

Tuesday, 3*d* July, 1744.

At 11 o'clock, this morning, the Governor, and all the honourable commissioners, had a meeting with the Six Nations in the court-house, when his Honour made a speech to them, as did the commissioners of Virginia and Maryland; and each party presented strings and belts of wampum; on receipt of which, the Indians gave the usual cry of approbation, and in a stronger and more cheerful tone than heretofore. They were served with plenty of rum at the conclusion of the speeches, and drank it with a good *goût.*[29]

Wednesday, 4th July, 1744.

The Indian chiefs assembled in the court-house, and the Governor and commissioners met them there, when the speeches made yesterday, by the latter gentlemen, were answered by the Indian orators. After this, the chiefs made a present of a large bundle of deer-skins to his Honour, the commissioners of Virginia, and to those of Maryland, which were kindly accepted. The Governor, commissioners of Virginia, and the white bystanders, gave three loud huzzas, and thereby put an end to the treaty in regard to them.

In the Afternoon. Court-House. . . .

Our commissioners shook the several chiefs by the hand, and took their leaves of them, presenting Gachradodon with a fine laced hat.

This Gachradodon is a very celebrated warrior, and one of the Cahuga chiefs, about forty years of age, tall, straight-limbed, and a graceful person, but not so fat as Cannasateego. His action, when he spoke, was certainly the most graceful, as well as bold, that any person ever saw; without the buffoonery of the French, or over-solemn deportment of the haughty Spaniards. When he made the complimentary speech . . . on the occasion of giving Lord Baltimore the name of Tocaryhogon, he was complimented by the Governor, who said, "that he would have made a good figure in the forum of old Rome." And Mr. Commissioner Jenings declared, "that he had never seen so just an action in any of the most celebrated orators he had heard speak." . . .

[29]*goût*: Relish or zest.

A Chronology of the Iroquois Peoples
and Their Neighbors
(c. 1300–1830s)

c.1300–
1450   Founding of the Iroquois League of Five Nations (Mohawks, Oneidas, Onondagas, Cayugas, and Senecas).

c.
1480s   European fishermen begin visiting the Grand Banks, spending time ashore and trading with natives.

1607   First permanent English colony, Virginia.

1608   Founding of New France.

1609   Henry Hudson sails up the river that is now named after him and trades with natives near modern-day Albany, New York.

1624   Dutch set up a trading post at Fort Orange, where Albany stands today. Council between Five Nations and New France leads to a trade agreement.

1626   Dutch found New Amsterdam, capital of the colony of New Netherland.

1643   First reference, in formal talks with the Dutch, to an "iron chain" linking Iroquois and colonists.

1664   In September, England takes over New Netherland, renames it "New York," and then holds a treaty with Iroquois envoys at Albany (formerly Fort Orange).

1677   Covenant Chain Confederation, with a "silver chain," forged between Iroquois and the "River Indians" of the Hudson Valley on the one hand and, on the other, New York, Connecticut, and Massachusetts. Ambassadors from Virginia and Maryland join New York Governor Sir Edmund Andros in making a second "Silver" Covenant Chain with Iroquois.

1682   Pennsylvania founded. William Penn meets with Delaware Indians, purchasing lands and promising peace, the first of many

127

treaty councils between Pennsylvania leaders and surrounding native peoples.

1683 In an agreement remembered at Lancaster in 1744, the Iroquois hand over the Susquehanna Valley to New York Governor Thomas Dongan in trust to prevent William Penn from purchasing it. (They deny having given or sold it to Dongan.)

1685 Virginia ambassador returns to Albany to arrange a corridor on the Virginia frontier where Iroquois war parties en route south can pass safely, an issue that will surface again at Lancaster in 1744.

**1689–
1697** England and France at war (in America called King William's War).

1701 First official contact between Pennsylvania and Iroquois occurs when an envoy from the Five Nations attends a conference between William Penn and natives living on the Pennsylvania frontier. Iroquois trade with Pennsylvanians grows. At a series of treaties at Onondaga (the Five Nations capital), Albany, and Montreal, Iroquois leaders make peace with England and France.

**1702–
1713** England and France again at war (War of the Spanish Succession or Queen Anne's War).

1710 Conrad Weiser, age thirteen, arrives from Germany with his family to settle on the New York frontier.

**1711–
1713** War between Tuscaroras and their North Carolina neighbors leads many Tuscarora refugees to move north toward the Iroquois.

**1712–
1713** Conrad Weiser, to ease the strain on the family's meager resources and to learn the language, goes to live among nearby Mohawks.

**c.
1720** Tuscaroras are formally made the sixth nation of the Iroquois League.

1722 Council at Albany between the Iroquois and New York, Virginia, and Pennsylvania. Differing interpretations of the treaty's results will surface at Lancaster in 1744.

1728 Iroquois presence at Pennsylvania treaty councils with Indians grows, led by the Oneida Shickellamy, who oversees the Six Nations' relationships with natives and colonists between Iroquois country and Pennsylvania settlements.

1729 Conrad Weiser moves to the Pennsylvania frontier.

1730 Town of Lancaster is founded.

1732 Cayuga, Seneca, and Oneida envoys meet with William Penn's son Thomas in Philadelphia. The two sides "light a fire" in the Pennsylvania capital where formal talks can be held in the future, and "clear a road" for diplomats to travel to that fire in peace. Shickellamy and Conrad Weiser are formally proclaimed the go-betweens for managing relations between peoples.

1736 A second major treaty in Philadelphia with the Iroquois and Proprietor Thomas Penn. Confirming the 1732 agreements, the two sides proclaim a "Chain of Friendship" and agree that only the Five Nations may speak formally for all the Indians living between Philadelphia and Onondaga. Iroquois surrender the Susquehanna Valley to the province and ask Penn's help with settling their land claims in Maryland.

1737 Infamous land grab called the "Walking Purchase": Claiming that Delawares had agreed to sell to the province as much land up the Delaware River as a man could "walk" in a day and a half, Proprietor Penn dispatches runners along cleared paths to cover far more ground than the Indians had meant to surrender.

1742 At a treaty in Philadelphia, Iroquois speaker Canassatego supports Pennsylvania's land dealings with Delawares and castigates Delaware leaders, telling them not to speak in diplomatic councils and ordering them to leave the disputed territory. An Iroquois war party skirmishes with Virginia frontiersmen, leading to fears of a wider war.

1743 Conrad Weiser and Shickellamy, along with naturalist William Bartram and cartographer Lewis Evans, travel to Onondaga to begin the process of healing the wounds caused by the skirmish, a process that would continue at Lancaster the following summer.

1744–
1748 War of the Austrian Succession (in America, called King George's War).

1744 Mohawk delegation visits Boston while other Iroquois envoys hold talks at Albany, and a third group, numbering some 250 men, women, and children, travels to Lancaster for talks with Pennsylvania, Maryland, and Virginia. Renewing the alliance, "burying the hatchet" of that 1742 skirmish in Virginia, the two sides also sign agreements settling Iroquois claims to lands in Virginia and Maryland.

1745 Virginia begins granting lands in the Ohio Valley, much farther west than the Iroquois thought they had relinquished at Lancaster.

1749 To block English expansion into Ohio, French troops march through the region, leaving behind lead plates claiming it for the King of France.

1750 Weiser visits Onondaga, finds Canassatego dead (perhaps assassinated) and pro-French Iroquois in control.

1754 France and England go to war over the Ohio Country, which soon becomes a world war between the two empires known as the Seven Years War or the French and Indian War. Native war parties attack across the colonial frontier.

1760 Conrad Weiser dies.

1763 British King George III issues a proclamation forbidding colonial settlement beyond the Appalachian Mountains; colonists resent and usually ignore this "Proclamation Line"; major Indian uprising in the Ohio Country, known as Pontiac's Rebellion.

1776 Declaration of Independence for the new United States of America. Both sides in the rebellion, British and American, try to win the Iroquois as allies in the struggle.

1777 Unable to agree among themselves as to the proper course to take, the Iroquois Confederacy breaks apart, with some favoring the rebels, some the Crown, and some neither.

1778–
1783 Brutal border war between rebels and Iroquois loyal to Britain. Many Iroquois move to Canada.

1784 Treaty of Fort Stanwix, during which the victorious United States attempts to end Iroquois sovereignty.

1780s–
1830s In a series of treaties, many of them fraudulent, New York state and the United States acquire most of the Iroquois lands. Iroquois reconstitute their government or "rekindle" their "council fire," one in Canada and one in upstate New York. Some Iroquois migrate to Wisconsin and other western lands.

Questions for Consideration

1. Why did Iroquois come to the council at Lancaster? What did they hope to gain from these talks? Did they get what they wanted?

2. Why did colonists come to the council at Lancaster? What did they hope to gain from these talks? Did they get what they wanted?

3. To what extent did the aspirations and the agendas of the two sides overlap and to what extent did they conflict?

4. Why did Benjamin Franklin publish the proceedings? What audience was he trying to reach? What impression of Native Americans would those readers—most of whom had little or no contact with Indians—have gained from reading Franklin's account?

5. Some scholars have concluded that the official treaty minutes are accurate representations of Native Americans speaking centuries ago, that in them we can truly hear Indian voices. Others disagree, arguing that many screens, or filters, exist between Iroquois orators speaking at Lancaster in 1744 and the words on the page before us today. Consider what some of those filters might be. How great might the distortion of Canassatego's words be?

6. Some scholars argue that the diplomatic game was played by Native American rules or, as Canassatego put it, "according to our Custom." Others conclude that European assumptions and forms can be found on every page and every day. Which argument do you find more credible, and why?

7. On July 4 Canassatego told colonists that Iroquois and the colonists were like one people: "You and we have but one Heart, one Head, one Eye, one Ear, and one Hand." Just a few days earlier, however, another Iroquois—Gachradodon—insisted that the two sides were fundamentally different. "The World at first was made on the other Side of the Great Water [the Atlantic Ocean] different from what it is on this Side," he proclaimed, "as may be known from the different Colours of our Skin . . . ; you have your Laws and Customs, and so have we." Can both Iroquois be right?

8. What was Conrad Weiser's role in the negotiations? Can you guess at his motivations? His true allegiance?

9. Is there evidence in these texts for Native Americans adopting some European customs? Of Europeans adopting some Native American customs?

10. Compare the Iroquois council held at Onondaga in August 1743 as described by John Bartram and Conrad Weiser (Documents 2 and 3) with the council convened with colonists at Lancaster the following summer (Part Two). Where are these proceedings similar and where are they different? How do you account for the similarities and differences you find?

11. Compare the official published account of the Lancaster Treaty by Benjamin Franklin (Part Two) with the unofficial—and, until 1800, unpublished—account written by Witham Marshe (Document 4). Where do these texts overlap, and where do they diverge? If you had to choose only one document to give a sense of what life was like when natives and colonists got together, which would you choose? Why?

12. The Introduction mentions that native women played a crucial role in diplomacy, one that few colonists noticed or understood. What did colonial men write about Iroquois women?

Selected Bibliography

Aquila, Richard. *The Iroquois Restoration: Iroquois Diplomacy on the Colonial Frontier, 1701–1754*. Detroit: Wayne State University Press, 1983.

Boyd, Julian P., ed. *Indian Treaties Printed by Benjamin Franklin, 1736–1762*. Philadelphia: The Historical Society of Pennsylvania, 1938.

Calloway, Colin G. *New Worlds for All: Indians, Europeans, and the Remaking of Early America*. Baltimore: Johns Hopkins University Press, 1997.

Cayton, Andrew R. L., and Fredrika Teute, eds. *Contact Points: American Frontiers from the Mohawk Valley to the Mississippi, 1750–1830*. Chapel Hill: University of North Carolina Press, 1998.

Colden, Cadwallader. *The History of the Five Indian Nations Depending on the Province of New-York in America*. Ithaca, N.Y.: Cornell University Press, 1958.

Dennis, Matthew. *Cultivating a Landscape of Peace: Iroquois-European Encounters in Seventeenth-Century America*. Ithaca, N.Y.: Cornell University Press, 1993.

Dowd, Gregory Evans. *A Spirited Resistance: The North American Indian Struggle for Unity, 1745–1815*. Baltimore: Johns Hopkins University Press, 1992.

———. *War under Heaven: Pontiac, the Indian Nations, and the British Empire*. Baltimore: Johns Hopkins University Press, 2002.

Fenton, William N. *The Great Law and the Longhouse: A Political History of the Iroquois Confederacy*. Norman: University of Oklahoma Press, 1998.

Gustafson, Sandra M. *Eloquence is Power: Oratory and Performance in Early America*. Chapel Hill: University of North Carolina Press, 2000.

Harper, Steven Craig. *Promised Land: Penn's Holy Experiment, The Walking Purchase, and the Dispossession of Delawares, 1600–1763*. Bethlehem, Pa.: Lehigh University Press, 2006.

Hauptman, Laurence M. *Conspiracy of Interests: Iroquois Dispossession and the Rise of New York State*. Syracuse, N.Y.: Syracuse University Press, 1999.

Hinderaker, Eric. *Elusive Empires: Constructing Colonialism in the Ohio Valley, 1673–1800*. New York: Cambridge University Press, 1997.

Jemison, G. Peter, and Anna M. Schein, eds. *Treaty of Canandaigua, 1794: 200 Years of Treaty Relations between the Iroquois Confederacy and the United States.* Santa Fe: Clear Light Publishers, 2000.

Jennings, Francis. *The Ambiguous Iroquois Empire: The Covenant Chain Confederation of Indian Tribes with English Colonies from Its Beginnings to the Lancaster Treaty of 1744.* New York: W. W. Norton, 1984.

————. *Empire of Fortune: Crowns, Colonies, and Tribes in the Seven Years War in America.* New York: W. W. Norton, 1988.

————, ed. *The History and Culture of Iroquois Diplomacy: An Interdisciplinary Guide to the Treaties of the Six Nations and Their League.* Syracuse, N.Y.: Syracuse University Press, 1985.

Jones, Dorothy V. *License for Empire: Colonialism by Treaty in Early America.* Chicago: University of Chicago Press, 1982.

Kalter, Susan, ed. *Benjamin Franklin, Pennsylvania, and the First Nations: The Treaties of 1736–62.* Urbana: University of Illinois Press, 2006.

Lyons, Oren, and John C. Mohawk, eds. *Exiled in the Land of the Free: Democracy, Indian Nations, and the U.S. Constitution.* Santa Fe: Clear Light Publishers, 1992.

Mancall, Peter C. *Deadly Medicine: Indians and Alcohol in Early America.* Ithaca, N.Y.: Cornell University Press, 1995.

————, and James H. Merrell, eds. *American Encounters: Natives and Newcomers from European Contact to Indian Removal, 1500–1850.* Second edition. New York: Routledge, 2007.

Mandell, Daniel R. *Behind the Frontier: Indians in Eighteenth-Century Massachusetts.* Lincoln: University of Nebraska Press, 1996.

Mann, Barbara Alice, ed. *Native American Speakers of the Eastern Woodlands: Selected Speeches and Critical Analyses.* Contributions to the Study of Mass Media and Communications, No. 60. Westport, Conn.: Greenwood Press, 2001.

Merrell, James H. *The Indians' New World: Catawbas and Their Neighbors from European Contact through the Era of Removal.* Chapel Hill: University of North Carolina Press, 1989.

————. *Into the American Woods: Negotiators on the Pennsylvania Frontier.* New York: W. W. Norton, 1999.

————. " 'I desire all that I have said . . . may be taken down aright': Revisiting Teedyuscung's 1756 Treaty Council Speeches." *William and Mary Quarterly,* Third Series, LXIII (October 2006): 777–826.

Merritt, Jane T. *At the Crossroads: Indians and Empires on a Mid-Atlantic Frontier, 1700–1763.* Chapel Hill: University of North Carolina Press, 2003.

Murray, David. *Forked Tongues: Speech, Writing, and Representation in North American Indian Texts.* Bloomington: Indiana University Press, 1991.

O'Brien, Jean M. *Dispossession by Degrees: Indian Land and Identity in Natick, Massachusetts, 1650–1790.* New York: Cambridge University Press, 1997.

Pencak, William A., and Daniel K. Richter, eds. *Friends and Enemies in Penn's Woods: Indians, Colonists, and the Racial Construction of Pennsylvania.* University Park: Pennsylvania State University Press, 2004.

Richter, Daniel K. *Facing East from Indian Country: A Native History of Early America.* Cambridge, Mass.: Harvard University Press, 2001.

———. *The Ordeal of the Longhouse: The Peoples of the Iroquois League in the Era of European Colonization.* Chapel Hill: University of North Carolina Press, 1992.

———, and James H. Merrell, eds. *Beyond the Covenant Chain: The Iroquois and Their Neighbors in Indian North America, 1600–1800.* University Park: Pennsylvania State University Press, 2003.

Rountree, Helen C. *Pocahontas's People: The Powhatan Indians of Virginia through Four Centuries.* Norman: University of Oklahoma Press, 1990.

Saunt, Claudio. *A New Order of Things: Property, Power, and the Transformation of the Creek Indians, 1733–1816.* New York: Cambridge University Press, 1999.

Shannon, Timothy J. *Indians and Colonists at the Crossroads of Empire: The Albany Congress of 1754.* Ithaca, N.Y.: Cornell University Press, 2000.

Shoemaker, Nancy. *A Strange Likeness: Becoming Red and White in Eighteenth-Century North America.* New York: Oxford University Press, 2004.

Silverman, David J. *Faith and Boundaries: Colonists, Christianity, and Community among the Wampanoag Indians of Martha's Vineyard, 1600–1871.* New York: Cambridge University Press, 2005.

Snow, Dean R. *The Iroquois.* Cambridge, Mass.: Blackwell Publishers, Inc., 1994.

Taylor, Alan. *The Divided Ground: Indians, Settlers, and the Northern Borderlands of the American Revolution.* New York: Alfred A. Knopf, 2006.

Vaughan, Alden T., gen. ed. *Early American Indian Documents: Treaties and Laws, 1607–1789.* 20 vols. Washington, D.C., and Bethesda and Frederick, Md.: University Publications of America, 1979–2004.

Wallace, Anthony F. C. *The Death and Rebirth of the Seneca.* New York: Alfred A. Knopf, 1970.

———. *King of the Delawares: Teedyuscung, 1700–1763.* Salem, N.H.: Ayer Company, 1984 [originally published 1949].

Wallace, Paul A. W. *Conrad Weiser, 1696–1760: Friend to Colonist and Mohawk.* Philadelphia: University of Pennsylvania Press, 1945.

White, Richard. *The Middle Ground: Indians, Empires, and Republics in the Great Lakes Region, 1650–1815.* New York: Cambridge University Press, 1991.

Williams, Robert A., Jr. *Linking Arms Together: American Indian Treaty Visions of Law and Peace, 1600–1800.* New York: Routledge, 1999.

Index

Ahookasoongh, 14
Albany, New York, 127
Albany treaties, 60–61, 65, 66, 67, 69, 127, 128, 129
alcohol
    consumption of, 115–16
    rum, 76–77, 81, 87
    toasting, 123n25
    toasting the royal family, 110n4
    wine, 114, 116, 123, 125
American colonies. *See also* colonists;
        Maryland; New York; Pennsylvania;
        Virginia
    Iroquois names for, xv–xvi
    map, 2f
    Native American relations with, 8–10
American Magazine, 43
Andros, Edmund, 127
Anglican (Episcopal) Church, 6f
Annapolis, Maryland, 15
Armstrong, John, murder of, 61–62, 73–74
arrows, 115, 125
Assaryquoa (Assarygoa) (Virginia), xvi, 44.
    See also Virginia

Bacchus, 114, 114n11
Baltimore, Lord, 68, 72, 122, 126
ban-jan (banyan), 121, 121n21
bar-lead, 64
Bartram, John
    background, 91
    chronology, 129
    "Observations on a Visit to Onondaga," 91–96
    Onondaga council and, viii, 94, 94n7, 97, 129
Beverly, William, 43, 113
Black Prince (Tachanuntie), 111, 118
Black, William, 114, 116
body painting, 111, 113, 125
Bouquet, Henry, 89–90
bows and arrows, 115
Boyd, Julian P., 39, 41

bumbo punch, 116, 116n14, 122
bumpers, 123, 123n25
burying the hatchet, 105, 129

cabins, Iroquois, 92–93, 110
Cachiadachse, 97
Caheshcarowanto (Caheshcarowano), 97, 98–99
calabash, 93
Caligh Wanorum (matters of great consequence), 10
Calvert, Benedict, 109, 109n1, 115
Calvert, Charles, 109n1
camblet coat, 88
Canada. *See also* Onantio/Onontio (Canada)
    attempt to divide colonists and Iroquois, 47
    British-French war and, 82
    Iroquois' move to, 130
    Iroquois name for, xvi, 111
    Iroquois relations with, 111
Canadagueany (Conodoguinet), 106, 106n10
Canassatego, 10, 13, 14, 15, 44, 122, 125, 126
    appreciation expressed by, 81, 88
    background, xiv
    on British-French war, 81–83
    camblet coat given to, 88
    chronology, 129–30
    closing speech, 30
    colonial culture and, 20
    death of, 31
    eloquence of, 1, 4, 29
    France and, 24
    Iroquois League and, 12–13
    Lancaster Treaty and, 1, 4, 26–27, 116, 117
    land claims and, 4, 13, 22–23, 51–56, 68, 72, 76–77
    language spoken by, 28
    leadership by, 20

136

Maryland land claims and, 51–56, 72
on murder of John Armstrong, 73–74
negotiation style, 48
Onondaga council and, 97–102
opening speech, 27, 110–11
on peace with colonists, 48–49, 68
physical description of, 1, 4
request for rum by, 86
unfair dealings and, 124
Virginia land claims and, 68, 76–77
Walking Purchase and, 22
Weiser and, 20, 31
welcoming song sung by, 110
Catawbas, 9, 23, 69–70, 79–80, 83–84, 107, 121
Caxhayion, 98, 98n5, 99
Cayugas (Cayogoes, Cahugas), xv, 1, 4, 11, 44, 71, 120, 127, 129
Chain of Friendship. *See also* Covenant Chain
Lancaster council and, 48, 58, 71
Maryland land claims and, 50, 63, 80, 84
Onondaga council and, 103, 104, 106
Philadelphia treaty and, 129
Virginia land payments and, 79, 80
Charles II, King, 50n8
Cherikees, 69, 70, 85, 106
children, Iroquois, 120
Church of England, 6f
clothing
given to Iroquois, 64, 88, 113, 126
worn by Iroquois diplomats, 112f, 113
worn by Iroquois people, 111
Cohongorontas, 56, 59
colonists. *See also* American colonies; *specific colonies*
chronology, 127–30
cultural differences with Native Americans, 21
desire for peace with Iroquois, 46–47, 75, 96
forbidden from settling beyond Appalachians, 130
Iroquois diplomatic rules and, 19
Iroquois names for, xv–xvi
land sales, 21
respect for Iroquois by, 4–5, 17, 30
skins given to, 85, 126
trade with Iroquois, 74–75
treaties with Native Americans, 15–21
Columbus, Christopher, 11
Colville, Thomas, 44
Conestogas, 9, 35n11, 69, 115
land sales by, 56
Conodoguinet (Canadagneny, Conedogwainet), 35n29, 52, 52n9
Conoys
colonist promise to prepare passes for, 86
ill treatment of, 74–76
Iroquois and, 13, 35n11, 59, 85
removal of, 75–76

conquest, right of, 59
Constitution, U.S., 37n64
Cookson, Thomas, 122–23, 122n23, 125
council bags, 17
council fire, 16, 108, 130
council house, 92
councils. *See also* Lancaster Treaty council; Onondaga council
engraving of, 89–90
etiquette, 26–27, 32–33
Iroquois attitudes toward, 94–95
Iroquois diplomatic rules for, 17
observations of, 91–96
present-day, 33
repeating discussion in, 48
U.S. disregard for, 32–33
women's roles in, 12, 28–29
Coursey, Henry, 65
Covenant Chain, 14, 32, 47, 48, 54, 78, 127. *See also* Chain of Friendship
Craddock, Thomas, 109, 109n1
Crazy Horse, 8
Cressap, Thomas, 68

dancing
by Iroquois, 114–15, 114n10, 116, 120, 125
by women, 118–19
deal-boards, 68
Declaration of Independence, 130
Deed, for Virginia land claims, 76–77
Deed, for Maryland land claims, 72, 124
Deer-buttons (Gus-ga-e-sá-ta), 95n10
deer-skins, given to colonists, 85, 126
Deganawidah, 11, 13, 17, 33
Delaware, 43
Delaware Indians
murder of fur traders by, 24, 61, 73–74
punishment of, 75
Shamokin and, 62n14
treaty council, 89–90
Walking Purchase and, 21–22, 129
diet, 94, 94n8
diplomacy. *See also* negotiation
as alternative to war, 11
Iroquois Confederacy and, 15–16, 19, 33
Iroquois League and, 10–15
Lancaster Treaty council and, vii–viii
Native Americans and, viii, 8
wampum and, viii, 11
Dongan, Thomas, 128
duffles (coarse cloth), 64
Dyionoagon, Henery, 113

"Eastern Door," 12
education, for Iroquois children, 80, 84
Edwards, Jonathan, 4
Ephrata Cloisters, 87n29
Evans, Lewis, 91, 94, 97, 129
evil spirits, protection against, 94n7, 101, 102–3, 105

Faces, Society of (*gagosa*), 94*n*7
Families in Mourning, 102
feasting
    Lancaster Treaty council, 71, 110, 116,
        117, 119, 122–23
    Onondaga council, 95–96, 99–100, 104
Feke, Robert, portrait of Benjamin Franklin
    by, 7*f*
Fenton, William N., 29
Five Nations. *See also* Iroquois Confederacy
    alliances, 14
    conquests by, 13
    Covenant Chain, 14, 32
    defined, xv
    establishment of, 12
    European explorers and, 14
flints, 64
Fort Stanwix, Treaty of, 130
France
    colonists and, 87
    Five Nations and, 14
    Indian wars with, 55–56
    Iroquois and, vii, 24, 47, 74, 79, 81–83,
        87
    Native Americans and, 24, 65–66, 86
    Ohio and, 130
    war with Great Britain, vii, 24, 31, 78, 81,
        82–83, 130
Franklin, Benjamin, viii, 4, 5, 19, 37*n*64, 39,
    41, 43, 108
    "Plan of Union" proposed by, 8
    portrait, 7*f*
    publication of Treaty proceedings by, 5,
        27
French and Indian War, 30, 130
French glasses, 81, 86
fruit trees, 92

Gachradodon
    background, xiv
    gold-laced hat given to, 88, 126
    language spoken by, 28
    on peace with colonists, 69–70, 71–72
    praised by colonists, 4
    treaty proceedings and, 28, 29
    "united nations" and, 12
gall, 103
games, 95
Gentleman's Magazine, 5
George II, King. *See also* Great King
        beyond the Water
    Iroquois allegiance to, 31
    Maryland land claims and, 50
    possession of Virginia by, 65
    power of, 70*n*25
George III, King, 130
Germans, at Lancaster Treaty council, 115
gold, as payment to Iroquois, 76, 80, 86
Gooch, William, 17, 20, 24
goût, 126, 126*n*29

Grand Council, 11, 12
Great Britain
    early relationships with Iroquois, 54–55
    Five Nations and, 14
    gifts given to Iroquois by, 55
    Iroquois land losses and, 50–51
    Iroquois support of, 24, 31, 46–47, 50–51,
        86
    possession of Virginia by, 65
    war with France, vii, 24, 31, 78, 81,
        82–83, 130
Great King beyond the Water. *See also*
        George II, King; Great Britain
    Iroquois allegiance to, 50, 86
    justice and, 53
    toast to, 87
Great League of Peace, 11
Great Ones, 10
great Spirit, 94
"Great Tree of Peace," 13
gun-powder, 64
guns, 55, 64, 115
Gus-ga-e-sá-ta (Deer-buttons), 95*n*10

half-thicks (cloth), 64
Hamilton, Alexander (Scottish physician),
    9–10, 15
Hamilton, Andrew, 117, 117*n*16
Hamilton, James, 118, 118*n*17
hatchets
    burying, 105, 129
    given to Iroquois, 55
    symbolism of, 113
    throwing, 115
Haudensaunee people, 11–12. *See also*
        Iroquois people
Hendrick, 112*f*, 113
Hiawatha, 11, 13, 17, 33
High Dutch (Germans), 115, 115*n*13
Hill, Aaron, 33
Holland, 14, 54, 127
homony (hominy), 92, 104
"house-corner people," 59
Howard, Lord of Effingham, xv, 65
Huault de Montmagny, Charles, xvi
Hudson, Henry, 127
"Huzza" expression, viii, 18, 29–30, 48*n*, 87,
        117, 123, 126

Independence Hall, Philadelphia, 9
Indian conflicts
    murder of John Armstrong, 61–62, 73–74
    in Virginia, 45–46
Indian corn, 93
Indian policy, 32
"Indians Giving a Talk to Colonel Bouquet . . .
        in Oct. 1764, The" (West), 89–90
*Indian Treaties Printed by Benjamin
        Franklin*, 39
    title page, 41*f*

Indian wars
  diplomacy *vs.*, 11
  following Lancaster Treaty, 30–31
Into the American Woods: Negotiators on the
  Pennsylvania Frontier (Merrell), ix
"iron chain," 127
Iroquoia
  economic problems of, 15
  establishment of, 11
Iroquois Confederacy
  American war for independence and, 32
  breakup of, 130
  cabins, 92–93, 110
  Canada and, 47
  Catawbas and, 69–70
  Cherikees and, 69, 70
  chronology, 127–30
  colonists' respect for, 4–5, 16, 30
  Conoys and, 59, 85
  control over Lancaster Treaty by, 15
  council etiquette, 26–27, 32–33
  councils, 5, 8–10
  Covenant Chain, 14, 32, 47, 48
  defined, xv
  descriptions of, 91
  diplomacy and, 15–16, 17, 33
  Faces, Society of, 94*n*7
  foreign policy of, 14
  France and, vii, 24, 47, 55–56, 74, 79,
    81–83, 87
  gold payment made to, 76, 80, 86
  goods given to, 64
  goodwill expressed toward, 46–47, 83
  Great Britain and, 46–47
  growth of, 13
  influence of, 37*n*64
  Iroquois League and, 13
  lands lost by, 30–32, 38*n*73, 50–51, 70,
    72, 124, 130
  languages spoken by, 28
  Lee and, 27
  length of claim to land, 4, 53–54
  map, 3*f*
  Maryland land claims, 13, 22, 49–56,
    63–64
  members of, 1
  names for colonies and colonial officials,
    xv–xvi
  nations of, xv
  New York and, 24
  origins of, 13
  payment for land in Maryland, 63–64,
    80
  payment for land in Virginia, 76–77, 79
  peaceful intent of, 48–49, 53, 68, 69,
    71–72, 75, 83, 85–86, 96, 104–8
  poverty of, 70, 85
  power of, 32
  relationship with Maryland, 71–72
  relationship with Pennsylvania, 15
  relationship with Virginia, 65–67
  release of land claims in Maryland, 72,
    124
  release of land claims in Virginia, 62–63,
    76–77, 79
  resistance of colonists to, 18
  right of conquest, 59
  role of, 13
  skins given by, 85, 126
  Thomas's expression of friendship with,
    77–81
  trade with, 74–75
  tree use, 91–92
  U.S. policy toward, 32
  Virginia land claims, 13, 22, 56–61,
    65–67, 68, 76–77
  Virginia school offer, 80, 84
  Walking Purchase and, 22
  wigwams, 110
  women's role in, 28–29
Iroquois language, 16
Iroquois League
  diplomacy and, 10–15
  establishment of, 10–11
  Iroquois Confederacy and, 13
  Lancaster Treaty and, 12–13
  role of, 12, 13
Iroquois League of Five Nations, 127
Iroquois people, 12, 62*n*14. *See also*
    Haudensaunee people
  accuracy of reporting of speeches, viii
  body painting, 111, 113, 125
  children, 120
  clothing given to, 126
  clothing of, 111
  dancing by, 114–15, 114*n*10, 116, 125
  diplomats, 112*f*, 113
  early relationships with British, 54–55
  eloquence of, 1, 4–5, 16, 17, 29, 126
  gifts given to, 55
  at Lancaster treaty discussions, vii
  migration of, 130
  origins of, 11–12
  present-day, 33
  restrictions on travel in Virginia, 66
  singing by, 115
  smoking by, 114, 115, 118
  Weiser's instructions on treatment of,
    111
Iroquois Society of Faces, 94*n*7

jack-pudding, 93, 93*n*5, 94*n*7
Jefferson, Thomas, 4
Jennings (Jenings), Edmund, 44, 116–17,
    118, 119, 126
Jenontowas (Jenontowanos), 106, 106*n*10
Jews harps, 64
"jo-hah" expression. *See* "Yo-hah"
    expression
Jonnhaty, 99, 100

"Journal of the Treaty Held with the Six Nations" (Marshe), 108–26
Juniata River, 75

Kanawas, 59
Kanonraron (Aaron Hill), 33
King, Robert, 44
King George's War, 36n52, 129
King William's War, 128
knives, 55

Lancaster, Pennsylvania, 129
  courthouse, 109–10
  as treaty site, vii
Lancaster Treaty, 25–27
  aftermath of, 29–34
  background of, vii, 21–25
  chronology, 127–30
  forgotten, 8
  Iroquois lands lost through, 30–32
  Iroquois misunderstanding of, 30
  land claims and, 13, 45–46
  legacy of, 8, 33–34
  major figures in, xiv–xvi
  significance of, vii, 24
Lancaster Treaty council
  alcohol served at, 110
  Canassatego's opening speech, 48–49
  celebration following, 29–30
  as "compelling theater," 10
  diplomacy and, vii–viii
  feasting at, 71, 110, 116, 117, 119, 122–23
  gathering of colonists and Iroquois for, 44–45, 109, 110–14
  Iroquois control over, 15
  Iroquois language used in, 16
  Iroquois League and, 12–13
  journal account of, 108–26
  Marshe's account of, viii, 108–26
  Maryland commissioners' statements, 49–52
  musical entertainment, 117
  negotiation and, 10
  place of discussions, 16
  preparation for, 25–26
  speaking order, 26–27
  Thomas's opening speech, 45–48
  timing of, 25–26
  "united Nations" at, 12, 71
  wampum and, 17
Lancaster Treaty proceedings
  accuracy of minutes of, viii, 27–29
  copies printed, 43
  descriptions of, viii
  Franklin's account of, viii, 27–28, 29
  as historical record, 27–29
  journal accounts of, 27–28
  language issues, 28
  publication of, viii, 5, 27–29, 39
  text, 39–88

title page, 42f, 43
transcripts of, 28
land claims/disputes
  Canassatego's concerns about, 48–49
  Chain of Friendship and, 50
  Conoy land losses, 74–76
  by Iroquois, 4, 21–23
  Iroquois claims to land in Maryland, 13, 22, 49–56, 63–64
  Iroquois land losses, 30–32, 38n73, 49–51, 70, 72, 124, 130
  Iroquois release of land claims in Maryland, 72, 124
  King of England and, 50–51, 50n8
  Lancaster Treaty and, 21–23, 45–46
  land price disagreements, 21–23
  land sales, 21
  length of Iroquois vs. British claims, 4, 53–54
  Maryland's payment for, 27, 63–64, 80, 119
  squatters, 21
  in Virginia, 13, 22, 56–61, 65–67, 68, 76–77
  Virginia's payment for, 62–63, 76–77, 79
  Walking Purchase, 21–22
land purchases
  from Cohongorontas, 56
  from Conestogas, 56
  individual states and, 56
  from Sasquahannah Indians, 55–56
Lee, Arthur, 32
Lee, Thomas, xiv, 25, 26, 30, 32, 43, 113, 118, 119
  Canassatego's criticism of, 27
Logan, James, 45, 57, 59, 108, 123
Logan, William, 123
London Magazine, 5
longhouses, 11–12, 33
lumber, 92

Marshe, Witham, viii
  "Journal of the Treaty Held with the Six Nations," 108–26
Maryland. See also Tocarry-hogan (Maryland)
  briefness of British claim to, 4, 53–54
  Chain of Friendship with, 84
  competition with Pennsylvania, 24–25
  designation of name for governor, 71
  Eastern Shore, 23
  Five Nations talks with, 14
  Iroquois claims to, 13, 22, 49–56, 63–64
  Iroquois friendship with, 71–72
  Iroquois name for, xvi
  Iroquois release of land claims in, 72, 124
  land disputes, 49–50, 53–56
  Onondaga council and, 107
  payment for Iroquois land, 27, 63–64, 80, 119
  Penn's concerns about, 25

Sasquahannah Indians and, 50
threats against Nanticokes, 23
Treaty negotiations, 44, 45, 49–51
treaty with Sasquahannah Indians, 50
Maryland commissioners
goods provided to Iroquois by, 119
Lancaster council and, vii, 1, 116–19,
122–26
Lancaster Treaty feasts and, 110
provisions provided by, 77
speaking order and, 26–27
treaty discussions, 49–52
match coats, 95, 95*n*9, 111, 111*n*6
medicine society, 94*n*7
Middle of the Hill agreement, 60
Mohawks, xv, 1, 11, 12, 13, 15, 20, 35*n*11,
112*f*, 113, 127, 128, 129
chronology, 127, 128, 129
Onondaga council and, 100, 101*n*7
Montour, Andrew, 121*n*22
Montour, Mrs. (Elisabeth or Isabelle Couc),
120–21, 120*n*19
murder
of fur traders in Pennsylvania, 24
of John Armstrong, 61–62, 73–74
justice for, 75
of Native Americans in Ohio, 73, 75
musical entertainment, 117, 118

Nanticokes
Iroquois and, 13, 35*n*11, 100, 108
Onondaga council and, 106–7
threats by Maryland against, 23
Narragansetts, 9
Native Americans. *See also specific peoples*
colonial relations with, 8–10
councils, 5, 8–10
cultural differences with colonists, 21
diplomacy and, viii, 8
France and, 24, 65–66, 86
ill treatment of, 73, 74–76
Indian conflicts, 45–46, 61–62, 73–74
Indian policy, 32
Indian wars, 11, 30–31
journal accounts of, 9–10
Lancaster Treaty and, 8–10
map, 3*f*
murder of, 73, 75
murder of John Armstrong by, 61–62,
73–74
praying Indians, 83
travelers' habits, 21
treaties with colonists, 15–21
visibility of, 9–10
women's roles, 12
negotiation. *See also* diplomacy
Iroquois custom and, 16
process *vs.* product of, 16
role of, 10
U.S. attitudes toward, 32
New Amsterdam, 127

New France, 14, 31, 127
New Netherland, 127
New York
acquisition of Iroquois land by, 130
Albany treaties, 60–61, 65, 66, 67, 69,
127, 128, 129
chronology, 127
competition with Pennsylvania, 24–25
Five Nations treaties with, 14
Iroquois and, 24
land agreements, 65
population growth, 31
Sasquahannah land purchases, 55–56
Virginia land disputes and, 57–59
Nittaruntaquaa, 101

"Observations on a Visit to Onondaga,"
(Bartram), 91–96
Ohio (Hohio), 87
chronology, 129–30
murder of Native Americans in, 73, 75
Onantio/Onontio (Canada), xvi, 111. *See
also* Canada
Onas (Pennsylvania), xv, 44. *See also*
Pennsylvania
Oneidas
chronology, 127, 128, 129
Iroquois and, xv, 1, 11, 12, 13, 44, 54
Onondaga council and, 100, 101*n*7, 102
Ongwehoenwe (men surpassing all other
men), 15, 26, 33
Onicknayqua, 26
Onondaga (Iroquois capital), 11, 15
councils, 31, 128
Onondaga council (1743)
council sessions, 12, 13, 129
feasting, 95–96, 99–100, 104
Iroquois attitudes toward, 94–95
Lancaster meeting scheduled during,
25–26
preliminary council, viii
reports on, 91–108
Virginia land claims and, 59
Weiser's trip to, 23
Onondagas (Onondagoes), xv, 1, 11, 44, 54,
127
Lancaster council and, 110, 120
Onondaga council and, 97, 100, 101, 108
Onontio/Onantio (Canada), xvi, 111. *See
also* Canada
oratory skill, 1, 4–5, 16, 17, 29, 126
Oughcarrydawy dionen Horarrawe, 101

Paine, Tom, 4
Pamunkeys, 9
Parks, William, 43
Penn, John, 21
Penn, Richard, 21
Penn, Thomas, 21–22, 25, 129
Penn, William, xv, 14, 21, 24, 78, 128
family, 6*f*, 21–22, 78, 108*n*12, 118*n*17

Pennsylvania
  chronology, 127–29
  competition of other colonies with, 24–25
  founding of, 127–28
  friendship with Iroquois, 77–81
  Iroquois land claims and, 52–53
  Iroquois name for, xv
  Iroquois negotiations with, 15
  Lancaster council and, 113, 117–18
  murder of fur traders in, by Delawares, 24
  Onondaga council and, 97, 99, 101–2, 104, 107
  population growth, 21, 31
  Walking Purchase, 22
Pennsylvania Assembly, 43
Pennsylvania commissioners
  Canassatego's response to, 47
  at Lancaster Treaty discussions, vii, 1
  Onondaga council and, 97, 99, 101–2, 104, 107
  Treaty negotiations, 44, 45
Pennsylvania Gazette, The, 7*f*, 39
Peters, Richard, xiv, 5, 18, 25, 29, 30, 88, 113*n*7
  notes on Treaty, 28
  portrait, 6*f*
  praise of Iroquois eloquence by, 5
Peters, William, 113
Philadelphia
  preliminary talks in, 25
  1742 treaty, 57, 129
Pilgrims, 8
pipes, at Lancaster council, 114, 115, 118
"Plan of Union" (Franklin), 8
Pocahontas, 8
Pontiac's Rebellion, 89, 130
Poor Richard's Almanac (Franklin), 7*f*
Potowmack River, 66, 68
Powhatans, 59*n*13
praying Indians, 83
Proclamation Line, 130
prothonatary, 122, 122*n*24
punch, 114, 116, 116*n*14, 119, 122

Queen Anne's War, 128

"Report on the Council Proceedings at Onondaga" (Weiser), 96–108
Richter, Daniel K., 11, 29
Rigbie, Nathan (Nathaniel), 120, 120*n*18, 123
River Indians, 127
Roman Catholicism, 83*n*28
roonan, roonaw, roona (Iroquois suffix), 59
rum
  at Lancaster council, 76–77, 81, 87
  at Onondaga council, 81
"Running Walk," 21–22

Sacajawea, 8
Sachdagughroonaws, 59
sachems
  defined, 11
  feasting with, 122
  gifts given to, 114
  at Lancaster Treaty council, 11, 13, 111, 113, 116
  land purchases and, 57
  Weiser's interpretation to, 123–24
Sagogsaanagechtheyky, 102, 102*n*8. *See also* Onondaga (Iroquois capital)
Sanderson, George, 72, 116, 124
sangree (sangria), 116, 116*n*14, 125
Saponis, 13, 35*n*11
Sasquahannah Indians. *See also* Susquehannah Indians
  Iroquois conquest of, 59
  land sales to New York, 55–56
  treaty with Maryland, 50
Sasquahannah River, 68
school, offered to Iroquois children, 80, 84
Sekacawone (Secacawoni) Indians, 59*n*13
Senecas
  chronology, 127, 129
  Iroquois and, xv, 1, 11, 12
  at Lancaster council, 44, 120
  Onondaga council and, 101*n*7, 106*n*10
  treaty council, 89–90
Seven Years War, 130
Shamokin, 62, 74, 91
Shawnees (Shawanaes), 23, 35*n*11, 62*n*14
  treaty council and, 87, 89–90
Shickellamy (Shickalamy, Shikellimo, Shukelemy), xiv, 91, 93, 94, 97, 98, 99, 100, 123–24, 128, 129
Shoemaker, Nancy, 17
silver chains, 54, 127
singing, by Iroquois, 115
Sitting Bull, 8
Six Nations. *See also* Iroquois Confederacy
  defined, xv
  diplomacy and, 15–16
  territorial claims of, 22–23
  Tuscaroras and, 13
  Weiser and, 20
skins, provided to colonists, 85, 126
Smith, John, 8, 59*n*13
smoking, at Lancaster council, 114, 115, 118
Sonnawantowano, 101
Spain, 79
Spotswood, Governor, 66
Squanto, 8
squatters, on Indian land, 21
"Standing Quiver" dance, 114*n*10
stomp dance, 114*n*10
strowds (strouds) (blankets), 55
Susquehannah Indians, 115. *See also* Conestogas; Sasquahannah Indians

Susquehanna River, 75*n*26. *See also* Sasquahannah River
Susquehanna Valley, 128

Tarachiawagon (Tarachawagon) (Weiser, Conrad), 29, 124, 124*n*28
   Iroquois praise of, 84
Tecumseh, 8
Tekarihoken (Togarg Hogon), xvi, 101. *See also* Maryland
Thomas, George
   background, xiv
   France and, 24
   friendship with Iroquois, 15, 77–81
   gifts given to Canassatego by, 49
   Iroquois land claims and, 52–53
   Lancaster council and, 30, 43, 45, 48, 52, 56, 58, 65, 71, 73, 81, 113, 117–18
   meeting with *sachems*, 118
   on murder of John Armstrong, 61–62
   opening speech, 16, 45–48
   praise of Iroquois eloquence by, xv
   Weiser and, 20, 23, 122
Thomas, Philip, 44
tobacco, 114, 115, 118
Tocanuntie (Tachanoontia, Tachanuntie, Tocammtie, Tocanontie), xv, 58–61, 98, 101, 104, 108, 111, 118
Tocarry-hogan (Maryland), xvi, 126. *See also* Maryland
   assignment of name, 71
Togarg Hogon (Tekarihoken), xvi, 101. *See also* Maryland
tomahawks, 113, 115, 125. *See also* hatchets
trade, 74–75
treaties
   as historical texts, 27–29
   U.S. policy and, 32
treaty councils. *See* councils
Treaty of Fort Stanwix, 130
trees, 91–92
Tulpehocken, 91
Tuscaroras (Tuscarroraws), xv, 1, 44, 60, 85, 101, 128
   Six Nations and, 13
Tutelos, 13, 59

"united Nations," 12, 71, 99, 102, 107
United Nations Human Rights Commission, 33
United States
   acquisition of Iroquois land by, 130
   Constitution, 37*n*64
   establishment of, 130
   Indian policy, 32

vermillion (red paint), 64
Virginia (Assaryquoa). *See also* Assaryquoa (Assarygoa) (Virginia)
   chronology, 127–29

competition with Pennsylvania, 24–25
deed for, 76–77
Virginia commissioners, 122–26
   Five Nations talks with, 14
   founding of, 127
   Gachradodon's views on, 69–70
   Indian conflicts in, 45–46
   Iroquois claims to, 13, 22, 58–61, 65–67
   Iroquois name for, xv
   Lancaster Treaty discussions, vii, 1, 116, 118, 119
   Lancaster Treaty feasts and, 110
   land agreements, 65
   land disputes and, 56–61, 57
   Onondaga council and, 97–108
   payment for Iroquois land claims, 62–63, 76–77, 79
   Peter's concerns about, 25
   possession of, by Great King, 65
   restriction of Iroquois travel in, 66
   speaking order and, 26–27
   Treaty negotiations, 44, 45

Walking Purchase, 21–22, 129
wampum, 16, 18*f*, 32, 54
   defined, 11
   diplomacy and, viii, 11
   Onondaga council and, 98
   significance of, 16, 17
   U.S. attitudes toward, 32
wampum belts, 19*f*, 32
   Lancaster council, 48, 49, 51, 53, 56, 58, 60, 61, 63, 78, 79, 80, 82, 83, 84, 85, 117, 118, 125
   made by women, 28
   Onondaga council, 95, 96, 102–4, 105
   present-day use of, 33
   role in Lancaster Treaty, 17–18
   significance of, 16
wampum strings, 16, 18*f*, 32
   Lancaster council, 117, 118, 125
   Lancaster Treaty, 49, 52, 57, 60, 62, 73, 74, 80, 81, 84, 87
   Onondaga council, 95, 101, 105, 106, 107
   role in Lancaster Treaty, 17
   symbolization of, 113
war dances, 114, 114*n*10, 120
War of Austrian Succession, 36*n*52, 129
War of the Spanish Succession, 128
warriors, 114, 125
Weiser, Conrad
   accused of tricking Iroquois, 31–32
   background, xiv
   beard, 87, 87*n*29
   Canassatego and, 20, 31
   chronology, 128–30
   efforts to please Iroquois, 26
   goods distributed to Iroquois by, 64
   Iroquois League and, 12–13
   knowledge of Iroquois by, 20, 111

Weiser, Conrad (*cont.*)
  Lancaster council and, 26–27, 45, 48, 49,
    56, 58, 61, 63, 65, 68, 69, 71, 72, 73,
    76, 77, 80, 81, 110, 113, 119, 122, 123,
    124
  languages spoken by, 28
  leadership by, 16, 17, 20, 29
  Maryland land payment and, 64
  Mohawks and, 113
  Onondaga council and, viii, 91, 93, 94, 95,
    96–108
  Pennsylvania officials and, 24
  "Report on the Council Proceedings at
    Onondaga," 96–108
  role of, 23, 24
  translation by, 4, 27, 29
West, Benjamin
  "Indians Giving a Talk to Colonel
    Bouquet . . . in Oct. 1764," 89–90
"Western Door," 12

White, Richard, 10
wigwams, 110
Williamsburg, Virginia, 9, 15
wine, 114, 116, 123, 125
Wollaston, John, portrait of Richard Peters
    by, 6*f*
women
  dancers, 118–19
  Iroquois councils and, 12, 28–29
  modesty of, 95
  Mrs. Montour, 120–21
  wampum belts made by, 28
Worrall's Inn, 115, 119, 122

"Yo-hah" expression, viii, 18, 29–30, 33, 48,
    49, 50, 51, 71, 78, 79, 85, 86, 87, 117,
    123, 125

Zila Woolien (Zilla Woolie, Zillawoolie), 100,
    101, 104, 107